Surely unto God all things return home.
The Holy Qur'an XLII

A PIETA FOR
THE DISPOSSESSED
THE GRACE OF PALESTINIANS

Aminta Marks

Grindstone Press

Library of Congress Catalog Card 93-080534
ISBN 0-9626898-2-3

ACKNOWLEDGEMENTS

"Up From Jordan" was published in *The New Laurel Review,* Spring, 1977, titled "On Coming Home", "Rug"appeared in *...a joyful noise* volume I, 1989. Historical names are spelled according to the *American Heritage Dictionary, 1985*.

I am grateful to Allen and Unwin Ltd. for permission to reproduce adapted quotations from *The Koran Interpreted* by Arthur Arberry, as they are quoted at the beginning and at the end of the lovely book, *The Noble Sanctuary , Portrait of a Holy Place in Arab Jerusalem* by Alistair Duncan.

The author gratefully acknowledges the invaluable and gracious assistance given to her by Jesse Washington and Margaret Bolton. In particular, the author wishes to thank Barbara Ajami for her sensitive and accurate editing, and Father Joseph Allen and John Marks for their critical readings.This book is printed by the Princeton Academic Press. Carol Jeffery, a dependable hand from the Princeton University Press, gave attentive and much appreciated guidance to an author struggling for the first time with the technical problems of book design.

CONTENTS

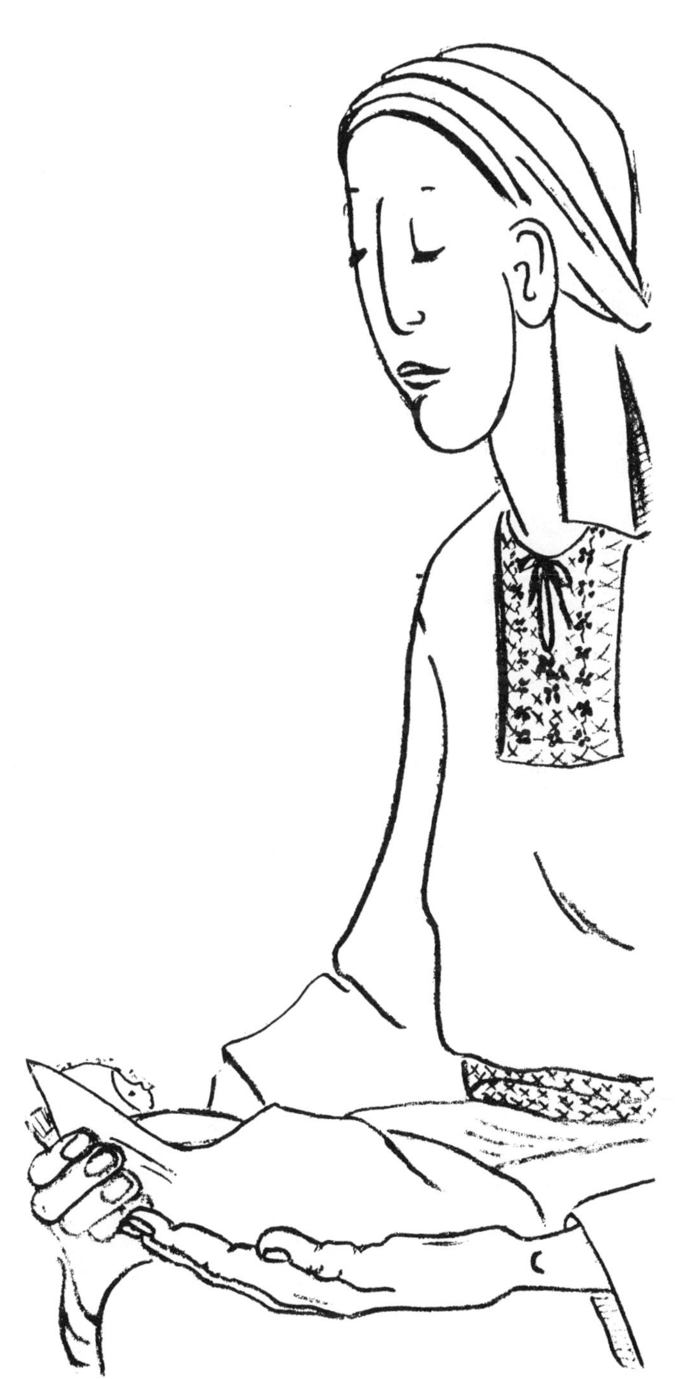

DEDICATION

This book is for the Palestinian women of the West Bank.

It is for Wadiah, who gave our family such love and tender care at the American School for Oriental Research. And it is for Mohammad's mother, the Muslim widow whose wisdom and strength made her family in Bethany wise and strong.

This book is for the mother of Majed Said, an assistant professor at Princeton University who died in 1958. He grew up in Taybeh, a village high on a hill in Samaria, a hill gray-green with olive trees. It is also for his sister, Munira,who was the gracious and energetic executive secretary of the American School in Jerusalem from 1967 until 1993.

And for Doris Selah, who was Director of the YWCA in Jerusalem in 1966-67, and, as far as I know, is yet. Under her competent leading, the dignified modern Arabesque YW building was completed shortly after 1967. There young Palestinian women still fashion lovely creches from pipe cleaners and bits of modern fabric. The figures round the manger look as if one could meet them on the street in the old city this very day. Who could say more of a people?

It is also for the many other Palestinian women, (Lizzie
Nasser, Asia Halaby, and her sister Sophie, to name a few)
who stayed in Jerusalem, fed the orphans, taught young
girls who were adrift on the streets the skills, the crafts, the
ways of women that their mothers would have taught them
had the war not cut down their culture. It was these women
who kept the city's grace when young men were forced to
seek work in distant countries: Kuwait, USA,Chili,England,
Egypt, wherever there was work to be done.

And finally, this book written from one side of the wall, is
for Judy, the little American girl who was once our
neighbor. Grown up and now the mother of grown
daughters, she has made her home on "the other side", kind
and hopeful that the lion shall lie down with the lamb.

INTRODUCTION

A study leave from Princeton University for the academic
year 1959-60 enabled me to take our family (my wife,
Aminta, and three children aged 5, 3, and 7 weeks) for a
year of work and travel in the Near East. Our headquarters
for most of the year were in East Jerusalem (then under
Jordanian control) at the American School for Oriental
Research, a center established by a consortium of American
Colleges, Theological Schools and Universities in 1900 "to
enable properly qualified persons to prosecute Biblical,
linguistic, archaeological, historical and other kindred
studies and reasearches under more favorable conditions
than can be secured at a distance from the Holy Land."
There, a stone's throw from Israel but virtually prevented
from visiting it, we entered painfully into the Palestinian's
plight of separation and alienation from their homeland. A
sabbatical leave seven years later, during which I was
director of the American School in Jerusalem, ended with the
six-day war: our hurried escape on the first day by taxi from
Jerusalem to Amman, our evacuation a week later by US
Army cargo plane from Amman to Tehran for one night, and
our flight the following day from Tehran to Athens.

Memories and impressions of those two years among the
Palestinians, shadowed by our direct and indirect contacts
during that time with Israeli and American friends in West
Jerusalem, are the centripetal and centrifugal forces acting to
produce the pictures that emerge in the works of this book.
Those two years loom in our memories as beacons of

warmth and understanding in a cold and muddled history of suffering and bloodshed.

John H. Marks
Princeton, NJ
October, 1993

FOR PALESTINIAN WOMEN

You want to bring them a gift,
And so you do.
You offer your writings
From the years when
Like seven-year locusts
Your family dropped down
To feed in the fields of Jordan.
Knowing interpretation to be
Restrictive,
You jot down images
In brief stanzas,
Little flutings,
Except for that week of June
In 1967.

For that week,
Wanting some limit, some exactitude,
You put down prose,
Unimpassioned,
Ordinary discourse,
As if to reassure
That the image, not being crystal,
Won't screech with scratching.

TREE

A pilgrim through Death Valley
Knows rains give forth
On west-facing mounts,
But on an east slope of Judah,
Beside the spun-wadi road
To Bethlehem,
An olive tree,
Gnarled and chance-twisted
As a protein molecule,
Old as the knowledge of good and evil,
Leafs out every spring.
God, it may be, flipped the poles,
Reversed our spin,
Knowing this tree would hang on.

Some people think
Eve didn't taste the apple,
But, of course, she did.
See how the increase of her law
Explodes like a yeast growth,
With the food for righting
Not near running out.

Imagine that she'd chosen
Fruit from the other tree
God put in the middle of the garden
Which, not forbidden,
Seemed self-evident to her.

When its fruit ripened, maidenly,
Mary did taste that untempting,
Raw umber grape,
And filled her lamp with its sweet oil.
Wondering at its pit,
She sequestered the promises
In sand
Where star-sprays watered them,
Pondering what they might bring forth.
Might! Indeed!

FIVE WEEKS BEFORE LEAVING
FOR JERUSALEM JORDAN

The yellow-green lights
Of new growth on the pine
Darken.
The spindled dogwood sheets
Wilt in the rain.
The baby turns inside me.

Its kicking, the calendar, the clock ticking,
Remind me that I should be packing.

In five weeks now we'll look down
From our plane at snow
Dazzling the dinosaur back of Swiss mountains.
Later we'll be walking with Peter and Fleur-
And a baby
Through valleys flooded with cow-bells' ringing.

Later yet, shielding the baby's eyes,
We'll strain to see the pyramids
Drifting in sand-locked mirage.
And the gold dome of Omar's Mosque.

But after, after all that, I'll be back to watch
Another Princeton spring
(Again a little sad that I can't hold
The greening caravan.)

FLIGHT #204

The blotched aluminum wing
Detached and unrelated cuts
Through aluminum fog
Which, blotting out
Beginning,
Blots out an end.

Wearing a hole
Through the gray-white shroud
We see a floating maple leaf
Outlined by wave-foam:
Nova Scotia profiles Canada.

Our spun-sugar ceiling
Dissolves
Topsy-turvy,
Stars burn up and stars burn down.

Then gray dawn.
And a meringue cloud over us
Floats on a sea-blue sky.
Under us a meringue cloud
Floats on a sky-blue sea.

Down's up, up's down.
The blotched aluminum wing
Fixed,
Transfixes us.

TURKEY

A Gypsy band
Walked the sparsely wooded pass
With a hand organ and a dancing bear
That got up on its hind legs, clapped,
And held out a fez as we drove past.

Now we see Ankara,
Her coal-tar,
Her bleary sunrise,
Her faded blue buildings,
The musclebound statue in her park.
We hear turbaned Turks grind
Gears and step on the gas.

A bull, though, shuttles the main street of the city,
Behind two clogging milkmaids
Wearing baggy pants and braids,
And a mother at the playground
Wraps her tarha close about her face.

OMAR

Omar makes good cookies
Omar makes good cookies
Omar laughs and jollies
Children with sweet goodies.

Over all the bumps through Yugoslavia,
Over roads black and snakey in the rain,
Over desert roads
Our children sang the brave refrain.
Finally we met Omar.

While I was hanging out the baby wash
Omar came to me with a news flash:

Last night Israelis killed two of our people near Ramallah.
Mrs. Marks, please tell the people in America.

Omar's father
Was a farmer.
He grew tangerines,
Oranges, dates, olives,
Cabbages and beans.

Every two weeks
He cut the waist-high leeks
And sold them to a monastery
In the Old City.

"This morning I read in the paper, Mrs. Marks,"
He called from the kitchen porch,
"That a Nazi club hung up a sign
'Death to the Jews'.
The government is seeking clues."

Omar dropped his soft brown eyes,
"I hope they don't find
Any of the men in that club, Mrs. Marks."

Trembling, stiff, I rebuked him.

"What would you do, Mrs. Marks,
If your home was knocked down?
If Fleur's feet were swollen?
And Peter cried for bread?"

(John was an hour late for dinner,
I was getting a headache.
Peter spilled ink
All over his coveralls.
I slapped him.)

Daoud lost a three-story house
And trees just greening,
Now with twenty-four dollars a month he's keeping

Seven children and a mute aunt.
The printer lost a new establishment
With fifteen unpacked machines.

Daoud's home now houses
An ambassador to Israel.

We hear the thunder. The rain falls somewhere else.
They make the Negev green
With water siphoned from our river.

Omar had a cow. Now he lives in the basement.
His children don't get butter.
His wife buys fruit by the kilo.

Omar makes good cookies
Omar makes good cookies
Omar laughs and jollies
Children with sweet goodies.

STATEMENT OF FAITH

The great dome of Omar
Like sun
Rises out
Of beige cliffs
Pocked with more doors
Than swallows bore,
And rather than
Taking up,
Gives
Space
To the crowded walled city.

Inside the mosque
A bowl of sky-blue tiles
Floats bedouin free
Possessing nothing.

Across the Via Dolorosa
The Church of the Holy Sepulchre
Crouches,
Heavy,
Claiming its plot.

The synagogue
Blocks forth a law tablet
Cast in cement.

It's the Dome of Omar
That shines to far-away hills
Telling the traveller
What city he approaches
From the wilderness.

An embassy flag
Though studded with stars
Can't put out the sun
Or darken the morning blue
Of Jerusalem,
City of David
Of Christ
Of Muhammad.

God help my unbelief.
Keep our stars
From signalling the night.

CHRISTMAS 1966

Against a jagged edge of sky
Judean hills knot up golden brown
And rose, until the sun tumbles down
Their far side, and blue inks deep,
Dashes near slopes, blots hill into sky-blue-black.
And star-thorns prickle over steeples and minarets
That pine the treeless silhouette.

Taybeh's unsheathed spires knife
The keen air that scores her mountain top
Where a boy's dream leapt off,
Ran the Phoenician Sea,
Then ran farther yet, where none alive
From Taybeh's cliff or from the softer plain
Can follow him.

Sammu's minaret too,
Needles the blue
Over her hill, though her house walls
Lie tumbled and her new widows
Salvage rocks from streets and goat pens
To build shelter from sharp winds
Cutting shivering children still crying.

Bethlehem's steeples sky
And run through a star.
Jerusalem's holy stakes spire
The height young men climb to die.

Rasp, winds, on the raw-throated bells,
Wail, Muezzin, over the crescent's driftcd trails,
Weep, Jew, on urine-stained extraneous walls.
Peace and love came down, but gone is gone.
Oh mourn. Oh mourn.
Still, still morn.

IN THE SUQ

Whew! zing! whew! zing!
Whew-zing-whew-zing-whew-zing-

Whew!
La'! la'! Bi-kaffi! That's enough!
Each time he wallops
The cotton
Blows a thundercloud
From seedy bolls
Stuffed into the corner
Of the stone stall in the suq.

"Just half of that will do-
"Nus-nus-half-min fadlo!"
She only wants to make a beard
For the Santa Peter cut out of cardboard
To hang on their door.
(Santa's beard should be sooty, says Peter)

The sorcerer parts his milkweedy mass,
"Nus? Bi-Kaffi? Enough? Yes?"
And picks up the cotton whopper again.

Whew, zing, whew, zing.
Flail. swell. quail.
He flails.
Cotton swells.
She quails.

Hoisting the bulging gunny sack
The American mother and little boy retreat
Through the curtain of red-checked kaffiyehs
The jinn has gathered over his door.

BYBLOS

While those with archeological minds
Clambered into the dank graves
(Not even drawings in the tomb
Could make me climb down)
I turned to the waves,
And clinking goblets with Akhenaton,
I lullabied Pom,
On a Roman column
Toppled to a brink of cliff hung
Over the fishing village,
To the metered wash of lapis water
Over a seal's-back slab of rock.

Fleur brought me a red anemone,
Yellow chicory, and grass-tender breezes.

BEDOUIN BOY

Under a Sunday-school sky
I stood on his stained-glass sand
Watching
A boy shepherd nestle a lamb,

Glad that Mike
Who's at nine and self-center,
Wouldn't snap
His last frame on people.

BIG FEET

We manicured western ladies
Pride ourselves on the petite dimensions
Of our extremities.
We protect them from the erosions
Of heat and cold and soap and acid
And from the stress that swells the knuckles
And makes the veins trace lurid
Patterns in strained hide
And carefully encase them inside
Pearl-buttoned gloves and shoes with fancy buckles.

But what promontories were Wadiah's feet
When she took off her lately-acquired
Shoes to scrub the floor or bake a sweet
On those late afternoons when she tired.
Her generous gnarled roots sprawled
On the cool stone floor as easily
As the suds puddled that lazily
Slopped from the pail she hauled.
They were as comfortably suited to her work
As the camel's pads to the desert's suck.
And her all-of-a-piece wide stride mocked
My twittery walk.

SASA

Sasa was poor.
Sasa talked too much.

Go away Sasa
We said.

Sasa shook her head.

Here is some wheat, Sasa.
Take it and go away.

Sasa shook her head.

Here is some bread, Sasa.
Take it and go away.

Sasa shook her head.

Here is a sweet, Sasa.
Take it and go away.

Sasa shook her head.
I don't want your wheat, she said.

I don't want your bread.
I don't want your sweet.
I want to talk.

WHAT OF IT

American,
I help God out of His botches.
Arabs say, "Ma'laysh"…
"It doesn't matter"…"It's all right."

When we first came to Jordan
I thought it was the slow sun
That so deliciously warmed,
        That was concerned
        Only with going its own way,
That softened the bones
        Of the people,
        That seduced them
        To follow his course,
        Splendid and slow
From night to night.

And Qassim,
        Telling about his baby Dalal
        Being burned on the leg and the arm
        When she tipped the pot off the primus
        They were sitting around
        Drinking tea,
Bit his lip when we showed concern
And reassured us, "Ma'laysh",
Though his eye leaked.

The donkey skeleton
        Lay white where
        The beast had toppled,
Its legs kicked stiff against the jeering sun.

The ass had thought
        He mattered.
        God!

AT THE WELL

Four women
At the Old Jericho spring
Pitched great sand-colored briqs
To their shoulders.
Then swaying their hips
To their laughing and talking,
They washed like a wave
To their camp.

*briq: large pitcher, urn

THE POTTER

Today the satin-eyed potter sits at his wheel
His lullaby wheel; the caress
The caress of smooth smooth rhythm
Waving wheat rhythm, the wheel's hum
The wheel' s hum and the unpointed rattle…
Shells rattle back to the circling wave,
Of the belt on the rim
The rim of the wheel…
The flywheel's an old clay jug!…fingers
Fingers move up the live form
Up the young pot over its long thigh
Over its compliant thigh over the warm
The warm swell and up the neck high
High up the neck where fingers fondly
Fondly fondle the hollow under the ear
And its curves pulse to the gentle
So gentle caress that smooths
Slow rhythm waving wheat rhythm until
Yielded completely
And simply
His for-dandelions vase stays still…
Slow rhythm waving wheat rhythm turning shy
Smiling at smiling shy children.

JORDAN SUN

25

Akhenaton and Nefertite
Caught sunshine
In goblets, and
Drank it.

Peter said, "I made a mud house
And I filled it with sunshine
And baked it."

JUDEAN HILL

The hill sits for her portrait
Necklaced in stone walls,
The loose folds
Of her rose-beige scarf
Caught in cedar combs.
Cut-block houses stud her belt
Where Bedouin tents once
Sashed her hips.

BEDOUIN

A Bedouin squats and scratches himself
Under his grand blue dome.
Near the goat-colored tabernacle
A child,
Horse-tail hair matted impervious,
Runs naked,
And a spare woman strides the noon-hot sand
In a blowing jallabiyya.
Not knowing propriety's lash,
A lone boy yells at his beast,
Then laughs,
Delight twinkling his teeth.
His toes match his soil.
In the beyond, a wool-gathering girl
With black-ice eyes
Floats on a cloud of sheep
Where camels crenelate the horizon
   (Their water, poured on the head, kills lice).

At the tel we stop
Beside men swinging picks
While basket boys
Like quavering lines of ants,
Jog up and down the hill
Singing.
We sip sugared tea, and at their break
Sit cross-legged with them around a mansif tray.

Then we return to our brick houses
And they to their diapason of sky.
Having trundled in their goofa baskets
A whole hill
Of an ancient city's shards,
They, like sheep and goats,
Know
The everlastingness of flocking,
With what God put on their backs,
Out to pasture.

Tel: hill, a mound of ruins, an archeological site
Mansif: a feast of lamb, rice , and yogurt

PASSING A JORDANIAN GARDEN IN MARCH
29

We walk up the dust hill from the Kidron
Spreading our fingers in the sun, cat-stretching.

Passing a gate, I smell wet mud.

Homesick, I tip over running sand,
Uncovering an orange crocus.

PEOPLE OF ISHMAEL

When she said it
I felt I was caught with the stone
In my hand,
Where we stood,
East
And West.
 I couldn't look in Wadiah's eyes.

"Maybe we deserve to be punished more."

When Wadiah's answer is deserving,
Grace can't save face.

WOMAN IN LUXOR

I wanted to tell her I didn't have time...
That our plane
Left in one hour,
So I asked the policeman
How to explain,
But he didn't understand
And told me to say "Shukran ikteer",
Or something like that, and I didn't know
I'd said just "Many thank you's"
Which in Arabic means simply "No".
Gentle and young,
She stood
In the caked-mud court by her door
Holding out a jug of her water.

I left her face
Dangling in the marcelled air
With my "Shukran ikteer".

FROM THE PLANE LEAVING LUXOR

The new moon's smile
Hung in the smoked blue.
Dawn waxed the horizon vermillion.
Some spatter flew
Sizzling into the Nile
And squirmed in the fur
That wrapped Luxor.

Wistful remember the Nubian boy.
His wax-glow face.
His morning's-now face.
Twelve-year-old swinging my suitcase
Flicking Peter a butterfly race.

A long time ago
I didn't pick a bloodroot
The plough spared
At the edge of the field.

BETHLEHEM RETRIBUTION

Having two pieces of embroidery
To sell for the woman
Wadiah told me her story,
The woman was old, near forty-five,
And four years ago, in winter, she found the baby
Wrapped in a bundle of rags, under an olive tree.
Not married, she had no child of her own,
And loving the foundling, asked the king
To say she could keep him for her son.

The king granted it,
At least until the child turned twelve.
By breaking her heart and her back for her treasure
The old woman brought him up to the age of four.
But the boys in the village, wanting their say,
Then began to speak up.

Here I'd better tell you that Wadiah says
When a girl does "something wrong" in this country
Her whole family, brothers, sisters, mother, father,
And usually all her cousins and connections
Are rejected, and probably hounded to death.
As if that's not enough, the girl herself
Has to marry the man, being nothing more
Than his whore, and God help her if she refuses.

I suppose, as a few people supposed before,
That's why some tender girl left her baby

Out there under the olive tree,
Thinking it was better for him as well as for her.
But probably most in town thought other thoughts.

In any case the woman had no help rearing
The little tad some mother
Was afraid to admit she bore,
And that's why she did the embroidery
And wanted to sell the handsome dress she made
When she'd still hoped to marry.

Well, as I said, with her small dowry
And the sewing she did each day
She managed to raise the boy
Till he was big enough to play outdoors.
It was then the boys began taunting
Asking him what it was the old woman
Had found under the olive tree.
They kept at him
Until,Wadiah said, last time I asked about him,
That the lady had had to put him in an orphanage
And she was living lonely as she had before.

The boys are smug as cats carved in jade.
Such a thing could have happened
In Bethlehem once before…
Had a father not made known his claim.

WADIAH'S PRACTICALITY

Flukes!
Had the Virgin
Drunk the old woman's potion,
It is true, she might
Have aborted The Son Of God.

Lord, pity us upright in our Rights,
Pity us stiffed in well-planned righteousness.

Nevertheless,
Knowing Truth's cussedness,

Because her niece's husband
Had to lift too many crushing rocks
That his fragile might might
Feed his wife and children,
Because he, too, had needs and a Right,
Because she had more faith in actual consequence
Than in the old woman's potion,
And, because she asked,
I showed Wadiah my diaphragm.

RUG

Here in the Kingdom of God
A certain wisdom shows where
Repetitions of a theme (with variations)
Play from an Afghan rug's inception
To where its pattern meets
Its last border. The artist repeats
The octagons and scorpions, but in one corner
Changes the color, interrupts the order
That's become too clear.
Knowing perfection flaunts his skill,
The desert dweller inserts an infernal
Eye, leaves a thickened knot, queers
The color of his dye.
Trusting the beauty of a fluke,
The spontaneity of a mistake,
The liveliness of tangled hair,
A Bedou keeps in the grace of God.

METAPHOR FOR GRACE

Joseph's in the shadows,
Out, in the darkness
(Not having borne the child).

He flushed, once,
Like the bush
In the wilderness,
And told as much.

Of his own free will
(As it is with fathers)
Joseph claimed
Mary's child for his.

Not he,
Certainly not she,
Wished to test his faith.

So, setting the mother
Nursing her offspring
On his beast,

He took the rope
And led them out
Of their own land,

Rose by night,
And took them
Out of Rama.

Oh, Our Father,
Of your hallowed will,
Claim us!

METAPHOR FOR GRACE II

And his father
Turned back,
Went the whole day's journey
Back
With the woman he trusted,
To find their boy
Who'd got himself left
Looking for answers.

O, Our Father,
Turn back
With us
To seek our questioning children.
A furrow
Sunders our eyes
That zig and zag
Roundabout as the Rachel,
Looking, looking.
Salt makes them smart.
Be merciful as Joseph.
Be as tender
To a mother.

*The Rachel: a ship in *Moby Dick*. Her captain's son has
fallen overboard, and she wanders the sea seeking him.

METAPHOR FOR GRACE III

All we know
Of the outsider,
The father,
Is three facts:
He registered in Bethlehem,
He made things,
He tended Mary and her son.

METAPHOR FOR GRACE IV

From the man
Hunched asleep
At the edge of the cave,
We learn a father's
Hard to identify.

Here, he stands off
When the wise men
Bring gifts to the child,

And in another scene
You can't tell for sure
If that's Joseph
Peering in the window.

But when Herod's jealousy
Bodes harm to Mary's child
The father
Walks out in front
Of the donkey,

Bearing mother and child
To safety.

From Joseph
We learn
What we learn in Beginning
From Abraham,

A father's faithfulness
To children he claims.
Abraham (being 100)
Is no more certain sire
To Isaac
Than Joseph to Mary's son.
And how many folks
Put stock
In a slave girl's claim?

But Abraham
Sends the servile Hagar
Away from Sarah
Whose possessive jealousy
Bodes harm to any rival
In her tent,
With provisions
And a father's promises,
Never once denying claim
To his desert child.

He loves Sarah,
But when the time comes
He tears Isaac, her God-given laughter,
From his mother's tent,
Knowing his son has to learn
The heft of a yoke,
He stacks wood on the boy's back.
It is the father, though,
Who bears
The pot of live coals

For altar fire.

So they trudge through wilderness
To the foot
Of Mt. Moriah,
Where Abraham bids his tribesmen wait
While father and son go up,
Promising their return.

After a short climb,
Isaac questions,
"Father, we have wood and fire,
But where is the lamb
For sacrifice?"
"God," says the old man,
"Provides".

And the two climb on,
Eyes darting,
Ears pricked up.
Still, on the mountain top
Isaac is the only firstborn
In his father's eyes.

So, child trusting father
Even past death,
Abraham binds Isaac's hands
And draws his knife.

Oh, what if…

What if the father grows
Enamored of the authenticity
Of sacrifice?

Grows single-eyed
To his obedience?

What if his eye
Doesn't stray
To catch the ram
Snagged by its horn?

What if Our Father
Is a Cyclops
Or the spacey eye of a pyramid
Looking straight out…

Not down into the thicket?

CHRISTMAS 1959

I suppose I'll go to Bethlehem
At Christmastime,
Smell the incense, watch the pageantry,
Hear the organ, see the tinseled tree,
Like one of those praying figures
They show in the Christmas pictures,
Pastel peaceful in a goldleaf frame.

Long ago, before we got busy
And hacked that frame together,
Mary,
Her belly stretched tender and hanging heavy,
Ground her teeth until the pain
In them throbbed in time
To the jog jog jog of the sore-skinned donkey.
Then she stood outside the dark door
In the cold Bethlehem air
      And the pain
      Came again.
So the steaming manure, the dusty hay
Seemed an almost comfortable place to stay.

      The mother whispered a lullaby
      Close by the baby's ear

And hoped he didn't hear
The ass bray, or know
What every mother's always known
And feared, that he's alone.
      (If the hermit wishes to imply
      He can be other than alone
      He lives a lie.)
Cling like a leech to the tit, wee one!

The sky blue veil was ripped aside
The night God died.
But we built a gold leaf frame
To fence the desert out at Christmastime,
We lit the incense pot in hopes
The rotten stench would drown in sweet,
We subdued the thunder in the organ's croon,
Trapped the lightening in the pine bough,
And tied the star down
With painted strings of gold to Bethlehem town,
And fed the poor so they wouldn't whine that way
To spoil the peace of Christmas Day.

      I almost hate the children I see
      Looking hungrily at me,
      Who let four or five flies
      Crawl on their runny eyes.

I suppose I'll go to Bethlehem
At Christmastime,
Even though, or *so*, the pageant hides the sores,
And tired women squat shivering outside closed
          Doors.

It is to such a town
That love comes down.

TWELFTH DAY OF CHRISTMAS
An account of Baptismal Day at the Jordan River

Ding Ding Dong, Ding Ding Ting Ting Dong.
The woman stood on the edge of the silhouetted disk
That floored the aether
Of the glazed tower,
And, poised like a gull to fly,
Clinked her bell against the tin blue sky.

Wadiah ran airborne under
The dong clanking,
Down the white stair,
Her black hair
Streaming us with her.
It was time for the bishop to go to the river.

Through the crowds gathered along the Jordan,
Shouting and clapping and ululating
We paraded popishly in the old Chevrolet
On the fins of the bishop's Cadillac,
Picnic basket shoved
Behind the seat.

"First," said Wadiah,"there's the praying.
Come, you're Americans, push right in.
(Then the mother with her daughters
Who had waited two hours made room for us
In front of them.)
But we soon grew tired of the incantation

And, squeezing out, Wadiah found a place
On the river bank.
People began to get into the scow that stood waiting.
They got in and got in
And then the bishop and priests
Climbed soberly into the same
Encumbered scow, and they tried to nudge it
Along its guy line out to the center
Of the brown current.
But it only settled itself.

So the bishop pulled up his hobble skirt
And bungled into a smaller boat, alert
Lest he drop his Bible, his cross, his flowers,
Or himself into unblessed waters.
(He got in. So did a priest.
A soldier came to grief).

Once in the middle, the ceremony
Began amid a buffoonery
Of juggling holy implements
And changing vestments
In the lurching chancery.

The cross was dipped three times,
People clapping and shouting and ululating,
And drinking the sludge
As though it were boiled.

When the boat came to shore
I thought all was done

Until I saw a young mother
Undressing a three or four month baby boy,
And watched the father joy in seeing
The bishop, his boat again pushed out,
Grasp the boy-child's tiny wrists
And dip him like a kitchen towel
Head and all
Three times
Into the cold river water.
And he went on, dunking
Eleven more who were
Drowned in the river and born again,
O-mouthed, chests popped out
Knees pulled up, fists grasping frantic.

On shore,
When the grasping child was delivered
To his mother's breast
The priest crossed oil on it eyes that it see
THE WORD OF GOD,
On its ears, that it hear THE WORD OF GOD,
On its hands that it work THE WORK OF GOD,
On its feet that it walk in THE WAY OF GOD,
On its heart, that it have the HEART OF GOD,
On its back that it BEAR THE CROSS OF GOD,
While the poor baby sobbed.

Wadiah's "Are you glad you came?"
Pushed a wobbly scow out into my waters.

PALESTINE SPRING

Almonds blossom, light as chiffon billowing
The cafe-au-lait fluting
Of the hills, whose petticoats show green
Over anemones, vermillion
In the dancing sun,
Like velvet slippers peeping
        From almond blossoms billowing.

A slit-eyed lizard changeling
Listens to a bedouin maiden's singing.
Applique on radiating sheen,
It lies stone-still on the desert stone.
Sky at the shoulder of the gown
Wavers a cedar fringe of spring
        Over almond blossoms billowing.

THE PROMISED LAND

When I first saw his hills, bare and honey colored
With not even moss or lichen, much less milk,
For food
And went into the town
And saw the blind and scarred
And lame and hungry and bored
People huddling against the sun
Inside corsetting walls laced
Too tight round the city's tumored waist,
All I could think was what to do
To corrode that awful copper glow
On the hills and make something grow.

But the sun has melted earnestness
Like honey or candle wax.
My flickering fingers now relax
In my lap and I smile and nod
And Arab-love the Promised Land. God
It's worn as raw as the donkeys' backs
Though! With piety.

ON THE ROAD TO ANKARA

Britannica describes the area:
"Formidable, with one major pass.
The main road
Runs through it
From Syria and Iraq
To Anatolia."
The family a nine-month-old,
A four-year-old, a five-year-old,
A mother, a father,
And a guest professor
Poured out of a 1959 Peugeot
For lunch and a diaper change
At the Cilician Gates,
It was hard for the mother
To believe
That Alexander used the pass;
That he made all the difference.

Our box-lunches were the regular:
One cheese, one peanut butter and jelly,
Carrot strips, and
The orange from Janin.

Sideways on the car's front seat, her feet
Dangling out the open door,
The mother opened a small can of Pet Milk,
Added it to the sterilized bottle of Karo-water,
And let the baby slurp and smack
While the other kids
Ran for a bit up rocks
Slicked by small rain.

The tree didn't talk,
No ghostly columns echoed
Through the canyon's mist.
No neigh whined in the still.
Even if the guest
Could have caught the snow peak
Quilted in fog,
There wasn't much for a camera.
The shocking pink almond in the cup
Below the road was too low,
And the streaked mud hills
Made the center strip too broad and dull.

But I'll never forget
The cold wet,
And the earth smell.

UP FROM JORDAN

With a squeal
The children lit
From the car cartwheel glad
On its spring.
Proper and shod
On the pool
Our feet too washed
In green grass.

That was in Izmir,
In the English school's compound.

Here, all is grass.
Everywhere
We wade in grass.
Grass is dewed, green,
Lush, compounded.
That other land is God's
(Call it honey, or gold, or brass. or flesh,
It's dust.)
Obviously, England
Belongs to men who tend
Their countryside more carefully,
Who keep the straying branches pruned,
Hedges clipped, meadows mown, song birds tuned,
Though they pretend prayerfully
That praise (a modest lie)
Belongs to Him on High.

CHRISTMAS 1967

There lapis lazuli
Was vibrant as that great-throated sky
Ringing
Over copper-crusted country.

Here the gem is muddied
By a slosh of greenery.
Cautious it looks, and workaday,
And earned: it's taken on an Anglo-Saxon air.

There tent skins are whipped
By straw-stiff wind
That brooms the bald peaks
And drops sand in the brine-tendered eyes
Of the twin babies Mohammad
And his wife carried from the on-falling wall
Of tanks and mortars and fearful noise.

There sleep
Is broken by light from a too-bright star,
Or the blaat of sheep.
Stones are food in the wilderness.
Winds are etchers,
And stoicism's dear.

In America
Mohammad could get work and buy a house
With a door against wind, and vitamin D,

But on Solomon's height, lapis lazuli is bright
As the potash sea, or the tear on Mary's lash.
Shepherds live in the rock's lea
Fluting the wind.

QUESTION PERIOD

Surely
They never meant to destroy
Gold in that greening time,
But holocausts, once they happen,
Explode like a dandelion,
Explode like a population
Into the third or fourth generation
And even Queen Noor is dumb
About Lebanon.

AVE MARIA

Holy Mary, Mother of God,
I wonder what you wanted
When, standing at the door,
You asked him to come out.
Were you remembering the time
He got left in the temple
And didn't miss you at all, until
You found him talking with his teachers?

When I joined you, out here, alone,
I remembered the child turned only his mother away.
But Joseph, too, spent three days
With you searching for his little son.
A good father Joseph must have been
To become The Metaphor.
I, too, married a good father
Who lightens my soul-searching way.

But, when you stood without him outside the door,
Holy Mother, and Jesus wouldn't come,
Saying his new-found friends
Were his mother and his brothers,
(And his father too?)
Could you be glad, as you knew
You should be, that he'd found
Another home, and saving work to do
Among strangers, and at least one of them
For sure, not even a Jew?

I wonder what you wanted, standing there.
Just to say "Hello, take care…"
As I do?

Holy Mary, Mother of God,
As I stand with you now,
Pray for me,
And , Oh, Pray for my son encircled in the crowd.
Pray your Son let mine abide…beside him.

Holy Mary, it's hard standing out
Here on the cold hillside with you, apart,
Remembering Jesus' giving you over
To an unfledged stranger.

Holy Mary, Mother of God
You know how dread steals into a mother's heart.
Ask your Son to take
Good care of mine.

DECEMBER 8, 1983

6:15 A.M,

There wasn't a lake or a puddle
To cause a reflection.
There wasn't a mirror.
It wasn't landing lights down
As I thought at first glance.
No, that bright star swung on the threads
Of the great swamp maple
In the V of its high crotch
Was double.

I asked you if you'd seen it.
You said "yes" as though
I'd asked another trivia question.
No one else seemed to be listening
For a song, and clouds came in.

So I saw it again only this morning
As I stood on the back porch
In the rose glow just before sunrise.
And again tried to hear.
A pink cloud did fly by, but too fast.

A pencil dredges things I don't know
Up from some chasm in my mind.
With the star stuck to my eyes
I pulled up Sirius, the Dog,… (in Egypt
Sothis, Creator of all green and growing things,
Who, rising with the Nile
Showed Pharaoh's star-gazers
The cycle of their floods,
Circumference of their years.)

I had seen well. Sothis is mated.
This is a year when the dancers break,
But only so far as to make me squint
Thinking my eyes gone astigmatic.

The letter writer must have seen this morning star
The night he slept on top of the pyramid
Just before the sun rose
And noisy tourists drove him down.
Sothis dangles us, East and West
Together on the fires of his dispersion.

Too blinded to sing, alone under this still sky
With the brightest star in the heavens
Flashing sunrise,
I hush, straining hope that the frayed hairs
Of the maple bow may draw from the star strings
One thin note of the angel's song.

JANUARY 1984, ALMOST NOON

It was the letter-writer
Who, that night on the pyramid,
Had (as I imagined)
Seen the star
That looks (as he says)
As if it's dividing,

Who, later, having sorted out
And clambered a winding way up Sinai
"Where God is supposed
To have given the Big Word,"
And caught up with the German,
Sitting, not even out of breath
From his straight-up climb ,
Waiting for the sun to rise,

Also got the word from the German
That our lop-sided star is Venus.

I could tell, he hated giving up
The Sothis tale as much as I.

Venus, I thought threadbare.
Anyone can point her out.
She has no companion,
She doesn't twinkle.
She's not dividing.
She's no connection to the Nile's flood,

The frequency of her transit
On the sun's cycle unmodulated
As the fall of Easter.

If I had my bird glasses,
Perhaps, Professor Jenkins says,
I could see that it's a crescent shape
That makes her light stick out
Toward the sun like pulled taffy.

But Venus is goddess of spring and love,
At the winter solstice,
Insha'allah, her phosphorus threads
Do dangle us, East and West,
Together on the fires of her dispersion.
Out of your question,
There where we got the Law,
I suppose there is a word.

Even when the data seem
Well settled on a name
For what you think you've seen,
You'd better check.
There is, more than likely,
A Pandemonium of fitting names
And most mislead.

But don't lose heart
When what fits is too familiar.
The threadbare evening star
You've seen rise out of the lake
To watch over the rock you've rested on
Since you were a child
Flies like lightning or Lucifer
Round back of the mountain
While you sleep,
And hauls up on her fishing line
A golden apple.

Even in our treadmill system,
What's lost its luster
May, at gift-time,
Shine with a brightness
You thought only wise men see.

GRACE AND TRUTH

The star-gazer told me something else:
Language is art, beauty, revelation.
To say is to make true.
There is One Word.
The Word is Allah.
The Word is Beginning Now and Ever Shall Be,
The blue tiles of the mosque,
Icon of the Believer,
Sacrament of one bent in prayer.

In Arabic
There's no presumption
Of pure reason
Nor of separate domains of knowledge,
No computer one or zero
Leads a mendicant
To take one fork
Or to predict his chances,
Having taken.
One Word has
Not one contradictory meaning,
(Like Cleave)
But, perhaps, ten.

Never having studied the language
I use it only like an American,
To provide my basic needs:
Blessing a friend,
Making someone welcome,
Saying "Thank you", "more", "enough",
"Half of that", "how much",
"Yes", "No",
"Please keep watch over my baby",
And to make certain
Someone knows where I am.

But to a bedouin,
At home in tracklessness
There's not a meaning not taken.

And that makes all the difference.

THE PROFESSOR

Once he would have been called an archer,
Now we know him as a gatherer.
Son of a Hagar,
His arrow, the breath of a bedouin,
Blows where it lists.

Near a second storey window,
In this gentle late-May breeze,
All the leaves in the canopy rise and fall
In waves of varied heights and lengths.
It's hard even to tell
Where the wind comes from
As it slips off the house,
Off bigger trees, wrapping around
Each solidity and undulating on.

The kindness of this air
Gives substance to things hoped for,
Gives evidence of things not seen,
As his air has in all its seasons.
Not too directed to wend a service course,
It's spread as wavery an awning of beneficence,
As all these springtime leaves
That lift and twist to catch more light for trees,
And lent, as these leaves do,
A quiet sweet, an energy
Sustaining life in the benevolent shrub
Of barren Beersheba.

And who can tell what, now,
His late spring breath will move upon
Veering off such homely stakes of foliage?

DONA NOBIS PACEM

Two events,
Paul's drowning
And the birth of the nun's baby
Happened in quick succession.
I couldn't utter a condolence.
I couldn't utter a greeting.

From his house
At the edge of no-man's land,
Looking down on the Jaffa Road,
Paul watched "their" cars slide down
The "Other Side",
The other side of the Judean summer glaze
To the cool, the blue-starched,
The blind-bright sea sharp with urchins.

In the evacuation, I saw Nancy,
Swallowed into the great plane's maw,
Raising her arms over her head,
Giving her twins the room they pushed for
Without crowding the three tots
Clinging to her bellying cotton dress.

Paul and Nancy,
Shipped out like Jonah,
Were belched up together
In a crook of the Ohio River.
But Paul went back and bought
Hanameel's field*.

The road from Anathoth to Jaffa was open.
The sea was waiting for him.

The impassive sea blinked,
Blind-bright blue, and swallowed.

Nancy's alone bringing up five children.

But heaven's not measured yet,
And earth's foundations aren't marked.
A nun and a priest gave up their habits.
Something new is created on earth.

A baby's born to a nun.

The mother, rocking a cradle
At the very break of day
Sings Brahm's Lullaby
As the muezzin's call to prayer
Floats on the land
Like a dove's song....

*a story in Jeremiah 32 in which evidence of ownership in
one's homeland brings hope.

LORD HAVE MERCY UPON US

A dark story flames
Like a candle on a stand.
Mary, the mother,
Jewess, and claimed,
Stands outside,
Turned away, irrelevant.

One woman's selfishness
(Not the Madonna's)
Makes all the difference.
Her laughter
Shrunk to grimace,
She reigns her lineage
Through the "sure side".

Matthew and Luke,
More radical than I thought,
Traced *Joseph's* lineage.
Rabble-rousers saw
The Son of David,
Pharisees saw
The Son of a concubine.

Sara's jealousy,
Her sending Hagar out,
Only *her* family *in* ,
Tents a ghetto,
Constricts a state.

Why, in manger scenes
Is *Joseph* pictured *out* ?

The sins of the mothers
Follow us.

FROM THE PLANE LEAVING AMMAN

The horny hoof nails
Of the lambs
Criss-cross trails up and down,
Back and forth,
Turn up little clouds of dust
Where He searches
Fresh green shoots
Out for His own purposes.

From the plane flying out,
I saw tracks like those
That check Judean hills
Again and again
On cloud mounds
Stretching low over land…
And over sea..

A REMINISCENCE OF PALESTINIANS:: THE WEST BANK 1966-1967

Written April 26, 1968, Post Scripts added 1993

I

July -December

On April 25, 1968, Anastasia Halaby went to jail. As we read the <u>New York Times</u> account of the women's march to protest the Israeli military parade through the Arab sector of Jerusalem, memories of the city reeled across our minds.

It was only a little more than a year ago that we waved farewell to Miss Halaby and the other diggers setting off from the American School for Oriental Research in Jerusalem on Professor Pritchard's archeological expedition to Tel es Saidia in the Jordan valley. While Aboud unrolled tent after tent to find four which wouldn't leak, and Father Huesman supervised the loading of the truck, the archeological novitiates huddled in the garage out of the weather, dejected. Snow, sleet-rain sloshed off the roofs down the necks of their slickers, and Omar the cook kept relaying dire reports of washed-out roads near Jerash. It was not propitious weather for a dig.

Then "Asia" Halaby swooped her Opal to a halt in the driveway, and everyone cheered. Climbing out of her car,

77

clad in an eye-brow-raised grin, a woolly sheep skin, a
straw hat tied under her chin, and good warm boots, she
heaved a bedroll, a stack of goofa baskets and mustereens
into her trunk, gathered her papers and sweet treats neatly
onto the rear window shelf and shooed everyone into the
proper car or Volkswagen bus. With no more ado, the
expedition was off.

A week later, Miss Halaby, in town to do errands, regaled
us at tea with tales of a sodden camp. Living conditions at
this dig were unusually dignified. Almost everyone lived in
houses rented from a nearby Arab agricultural project. Since
it seldom rains in Jordan, the fact that the mud roofs leaked
had gone unnoticed. That week, the soup was diluted with
the plink-plink-plink of rain dripping through the roof. For
the second night, Father Philip King gallantly gave "Asia"
his woolen stocking cap because she was disconcerted by
the plink-plink-plink on her head. Next morning she wrung
the hat out and returned it to its owner. At the dig, balks
were washed away, their valuable evidence sloshed into
oblivion, and most of the week was spent waiting for the
rain to stop. But Asia Halaby laughed at the men wringing
out their socks to go to bed, and spent the time getting
everything in readiness for the first ray of sunshine. She
also gathered a sheaf of tales. "Dig" stories are coveted in
Jordan because everyone, Arab and Western, rich and poor,
is an archeological buff. Those we met at cocktail parties had
invariably been to visit the most contemporary site and
followed the discoveries with keen interest. The men we
met in the villages had invariably dug at a site near their
homes. The earth was their history book.

Anastasia Halaby is an old friend of the American School where we lived from July 1,1966 until June 6, 1967 during John's term as Director. In 1948, just after the Arab-Israeli war, while she lived at the school for several months after she and her sister had had to leave their home "on the other side", Asia was acting secretary and liaison between the Americans and the Arabs. She was one of a group of perhaps twenty Arab refugees, friends of the school, who were given shelter and food within the compound until they could find some place to live in the divided city. Now she lives with her sister in their new house across from the Palestinian Archeological Museum.

These women accomplished a great deal in twenty years. "Asia", the one full of energy, during the late nineteen-forties and fifties, piloted the biweekly convoy of Israeli troop replacements through the Mandelbaum Gate to the Mt. Scopus enclave about two miles inside the Arab sector which the Israelis refused to relinquish after the 1948 armistice. That enclave was the former site of Hebrew University and Hadassah Hospital. Its high point over Jerusalem made it, also, an ideal military post.

In the same period, Asia started a project to give refugee women a trade. Finding that their depression over losing their homes to the Israelis was causing the women to forget their traditional skills, she began classes to teach again the ancient embroidery patterns that had once made their dress and household fabrics so distinctively beautiful. A few years later, when the sisters' new house was finished, the bright lower floor was given over to a refugee workshop. Here girls worked at well-lit tables decorating aprons, table cloths, dresses, book marks, place mats, and the like with time honored Arab stars, camels, flowers, shepherds. Asia scoured the villages and museums to find forgotten or little-known designs and colors, graphed them for counted-thread embroidery patterns, and bought fine linen and good Arab cotton for the girls to work on.

The third floor of their house was turned into a gallery for her sister's water-colors. Sophie had studied in Paris during the nineteen-thirties, though she did not find her style until she came back to her beloved golden hills and rocks. The green of France surfeited her, and formal European tulips and too-symmetrical bouquets bored her. When she returned to the muted tones of her homeland, her paintings of rose-gold landscapes and desert flowers bent in the wind became coveted by both Westerners and Arabs.

Between their two art centers, the sisters made their home on the second floor, which, at least until Israeli troops were billeted there in the June War, was one of the most attractive in the city. Curtains were fashioned from heavily embroidered strips that Damascus men wear for belts. Old Druze chests nested modern furniture into comfortable groups. The dining table was always gay with Asia's embroidered mats, and with Russian cakes and tortes.

The sisters were the daughters of White Russians who had come with thousands of others to make the Holy Land their home when they were driven out of Russia during the

Revolution. Refugees are not new to this land. Armenians
flocked there and were sheltered after their bloody conflict
with the Turks in the early part of this century. Jews were
given a home in the Middle Ages when they were driven
from Europe during the Inquisition. Even the Crusaders
found homes in the land they came to wrest from the
heathen. Arabs not only pride themselves on their
hospitality, but that hospitality is an absolute requirement of
both their Muslim and Christian moral codes, and homeless
people for centuries have flung themselves upon their grace.

There is a romantic story about Professor Howard Crosby
Butler from Princeton University, an archeologist in Syria in
the early part of this century, which is said to be true. His
group of newcomers to the Middle East was encamped
around a fire when they noticed a band of armed Arabs
coming upon them with their muskets raised. Without
hesitating, Butler did the only thing that could possibly have
helped the trespassers; he jumped on his own horse and rode
out to meet the attackers waving his arms so they could see
he was unarmed and calling out in Arabic, "We are your
guests, we are your guests…" The Arabs put down their
guns and, after inspecting the party, joined them for coffee.

(Post Script: 1993: Just this week a good friend asked if it
isn't true that the Koran not only advocates Jihad, or Holy
War, fighting for Allah, but promises an immediate
translation to Heaven in the event that one is killed in the
Godly battle . I had to answer that that is quite true. But I
went on to say that a Muslim also considers it blasphemy to
think he knows the will of Allah. Muslim rug makers make

intentional mistakes in the patterns in their rugs lest they
appear to think they know the pattern or presume to attain
perfection which belongs to God alone.

Mohammad's personal disciples joined to fight back against
those who were harassing him only after intense and warlike
ugliness began to drown out his message of complete
submission to Allah .

The Koran requires one to fight only in response to attack,
and, then, with the knowledge that Allah alone knows His
own will, presuming to act only in the unwavering trust that
Allah is unwaveringly merciful.

Moreover, to the Muslim, as it is to the Christian,
war may be a metaphor for overcoming personal evil.)

I am never in a tourist city without feeling sorry for tourists.
Poor things, we come, we whip around in cabs, we gorge
ourselves in posh hotels, we lug cameras to every
"attraction" and squint through pin-hole apertures at every
four-star wonder, we drag all our bargains-from- the-bazaars
through customs lines, and become thoroughly sated with
sights and guides trying to please seemingly insatiable
strangers. There is no time for a tourist to dawdle over all
the leisurely cups of coffee or tea or wine, or even clear
spring water, one must drink to enjoy the people of a city.
With a year in Jordan we could sip many cups of coffee,
many cups of kindness, and the pleasure of new friends in a
new land.

One of our first visits in 1966 was to the Halaby's house.
Here we reminisced about our visit seven years before when
our children were tiny-tinies. Asia's homemade liqueur, the
cherries from her own tree, was delicious. Both of the
sisters spoke English almost without an accent so
conversation could be spontaneous and bright. Often, it
turned to the problems of the country. At first I was
surprised that tension between Israel and West Bank Jordan
was so much higher than it was when we were there in 1959-
60. Eight years ago, we joked about the dynamiting when a
street was being repaired. In 1966, joking had stopped.

Then , the Samu incident occurred. We were invited to a
dinner on a November Sunday at Bir Zeit College which lay
near the armistice line west of Ramallah. We went, and so
did all of those invited. Arabs are stoic in a crisis, like the
British. Everyone mentioned the attack that the Israeli army
had made on the little Arab village of Samu which lay well
within the Jordanian border. The Arab Legion troops who
responded to the invasion, were ambushed and fired upon
when the Israeli net trapped the last of the rescuers hurrying
to the aid of the villagers. The invasion had occurred just at
the end of the Jewish Sabbath. Everyone hoped it wouldn't
go further. Everyone left immediately after dinner to get to
their children and families, for fear it would.

It was not until the May 1967 celebration of Israeli
independence that I began to understand the reason for the
mounting tension. Underneath the great red Star of David
which hung over the Jordanian sector from the old university
building on Mt. Scopus during every Jewish holiday, a great

"19" two stories high jeered in new brashness over the Old
City. One realized "20" was next, that eras are reckoned in
decades, that the approach of the end of an era was
ominously at hand. Israel was ready, even eager, it seemed,
to complete its task, to take the rest of the "Promised Land"
we had seen shaded on their maps, all the land "between the
two great rivers" as the Old Testament God had promised
Abraham.

On the evening of the anniversary celebration, my husband
and I took a walk. The Arab streets were empty, the shops
shuttered. A great silence held its breath. The stadium lay
on the other side, and beyond its wall, the home team had
scored the goal. The music, the cheering, the roar of
machines, and the explosions of the most dramatic exhibition
of fireworks I had ever witnessed rising high into the sky
and veering over our heads, over East Jerusalem as Israeli
reconnaisance planes often did, struck fear even into our
Western hearts. *We* were on the outside.

But after November, and before May,came December , and
Ramadan, when thousands of buses arrived from Turkey
and Yugoslavia, from Iran and Syria and Iraq, windows and
doors bulging with pilgrims stopping at the holy site in
Jerusalem where Muhammad is said to have mounted a
stairway of light and ascended into Heaven to receive
instructions for himself and his followers before he was
miraculously returned to Mecca. The pilgims were
themselves stopping at the Holy Rock as Muhammad had
done, to pray before they, too, made their way to Mecca.
For two weeks the city bustled with thousands of humble

visitors trading rugs and copper pots for food, cooking over campfires by the road. The muezzin's song seemed buoyed by the faithfulness, and on every sidewalk, under every tree, beside every wall, thousands bowed five times a day toward Mecca.

Then came Christmas, and Christian tourists flocked to the city, to their holy sites; bells rang, carols were sung, and somehow peace survived through Easter.

And we could drink coffee and visit and share in all of the holidays, in all the different ways of living, in the unquenchable happy spirit of the Palestinians.

II

January-May

1. A Mansif

Omar was the chief cook at the American School. Just before the beginning of Ramadan he invited us to a mensif, the traditional meal Arabs prepare for their guests. It takes all day to prepare, and one must spend a long, long time eating it.

Omar built his house in Bethany in 1961 or 1962 with the seventy dollars monthly salary he was then paid by the school. A solid stone house the same tawny color as the land, its large front porch, cantilevered off the steep hill under the main Jericho road, overlooked the Old City walls. To the East, hills and valleys ruffled away to the Dead Sea, a chip of lapis lazuli in a wrinkle of the hills. When we arrived Omar met us on the road and escorted us down the steep pitch to his house.

We all sat down to talk in an outer room. All the chairs were neatly lined Arab-style around the walls. Small copper coffee tables were placed in front of several of the chairs. Omar speaks good English, and since many of us at his party had been at the school before, we told story after story of people we knew and things they had done. Omar had worked at the school for twenty-five years so he kept many of us in touch with each other.

The mensif was served in the interior of the six-room house. Omar seated us, Western style, around a table and provided us with forks and knives. The enormous mensif tray took up the whole center of the table. Our host showed us that we must dig deep into the steaming mixture of rice and lamb to get the bread soaked in broth hiding at the bottom. His nephew joined us, but he preferred to eat Arab-style, with his fingers. It is fascinating that each culture has its own impeccable manners. When our children eat with their fingers it is a messy, glutinous procedure. An Arab, however, can gather a bite-sized bit of rice and lamb into his fingers, deftly roll it into a ball with one flick of his wrist, and pop it into his mouth without touching his clean fingers to his mouth, dripping a drop of broth, or even dipping his flowing sleeve into the dish.

We ate and ate, and talked and talked. Finally Omar passed
a bowl of fruit, the gigantic sweet oranges Palestinians grow
in Janin and Jericho, and tasty little bananas. The wealth of
fresh fruit grown in the Jordan Valley and in the mere tip of
the Valley of Esdraelon that is left to the West Bank north of
Samaria,- oranges, grapes, bananas, apricots, figs, dates,
peaches, lemons- was one of the joys of life in Jordan.

All the while, Omar's cheery wife came and went, and the
two littlest of their children peeped around doors or came in
to greet us, to bring some goodie, or get one from us. All
round and rosy-tan and bright-eyed, they enjoyed the party
as much as we did. Before we left, Nadia, the oldest
daughter, a student at the German high school, came in and
talked to us in English for a few minutes. When we were at
the American School in 1960, Omar lived in an apartment at
the school and his children and ours played together every
day. I wished our Fleur and Peter had not been in school
and had come with us to meet their old friends again. Walid
and Mufid, teen-age boys who go to the French high school,
also came in and talked to us, again in English, for a few
minutes. It was hard to believe they were the same people as
the little fellows who had helped Fleur and Peter put gravel
and sticks into our Peugeot's gas tank eight years before!

Finally, late in the day, we shook hands with all the family,
and, turning to the gracious Arabic farewell words for
parting, we climbed up the hill to our cars and wound our
way back to the school.

2. Ramadan Sweets

At the end of Ramadan, Abu Mahmoud, the roly-poly
youngest man on the American School staff, invited us to his
house to share some of the Ramadan pastries his wife had
made. At four o'clock one afternoon, we started off. Our
whole family, John and I, and Peter (13), Fleur (12), and
Pom (8), were loaded into our Volkswagen with Abu
Mahmoud and a jug of cold boiled water for lemonade.
Jerusalem water is pure but where Abu Mahmoud lived,
running water was not always available. He wanted to give
us lemonade that day, fresh lemonade made with lemons
from his own tree.

He lived in Bethany higher on the same hill as Omar. He
rented his house, but it, too, is of native stone with a great
porch overlooking, on one side, the descent to the Dead Sea,
and on the other, the Mosque of Omar.

I was a little afraid the heavily loaded car would somersault
off the steep grade of the dirt road that was made for goats
and shepherds. The car proved, however to be part goat, and
all the children in the village gathered to watch us park it by
Abu Mahmoud's house.

We went inside where his wife, his five children, and his
mother and father awaited our arrival. In the middle of the
circle of chairs was the kerosene stove the school had
discarded. It was the only heat in the house now clammy in
the late rainy season, and I for one, was glad John had been

generous with the stoves. At this house, only Abu
Mahmoud's father spoke English, but it didn't seem to
matter. The children enjoyed each other and fed each other
cookies, and John and I employed the few Arabic phrases
we knew to make some rough sort of communication while
Abu Mahmoud's infectious delight smoothed away all of our
embarrassment. First his wife went to the adjoining room
and fixed the lemonade. While Abu Mahmoud helped her,
we visited with his parents. Then they brought out the
Ramadan goodies. There were sweet-dough rolls, heavier
than most American bread, but good, and thick sweet
pancakes rolled around an oozing syrup and nut filling
which brought much satisfaction to our children. Abu
Mahmoud's wife was like a shepherd girl, young and lithe
and happy. She enjoyed his mother and father and both she
and Abu Mahmoud, though the parents of five children,
seemed still to be children themselves, glad to have a father
and mother to advise them and help care for their family.

When we had finished coffee we walked a short way down
the hill to the father's house where Abu Mahmoud's sister
was in bed. She had had a baby a month before by
Caesarian section, a Western medical innovation, and was
obviously anxious to have the assurance of a Western
mother that her recovery was as it should be. Western
medicine is sometimes difficult to accept, as is any foreign
importation into any culture.

Although uneducated Arabs find it hard to trust Western
medicine and hospitals,we personally found Arab doctors to
be excellent, and we entrusted our children to their care and

their hospitals with every confidence. Drs. Majaj and
Khatibi, both educated at the American University in Beirut,
are two of the best pediatricians I know. To our sorrow,
their hospital on the Mount of Olives was caught in cross-
fire in the Six-Day War and badly damaged. Augusta
Victoria was an old German-Lutheran school that the
Palestinians had turned into a hospital. The elegant size of
the rooms, the wide stone halls, and the courtyard made a
cumbersome but friendly institution. We rushed our
youngest child there one night with a fever of 105°, and he
received such good care that I was relaxed enough in the
morning to watch the sunrise over the Dead Sea from his
third-floor room… the third floor which was almost entirely
destroyed by Israeli shells.

The following day Pommy, who apparently had had a sun
stroke, was recovered, but Dr. Majaj kept him three days,
performing several tests to make sure he hadn't contracted
one of the Oriental diseases that attack Westerners. In the
course of the stay I learned about the new laboratory Dr.
Majaj was setting up to carry on his scientific investigations.
He is well known in the medical world for having linked a
specific type of anemia to malnutrition. During his earlier
investigations, his laboratory had been the refugee camps he
tended.

I was able to reassure Abu Mahmoud's sister, to cuddle her
baby a bit, and learn something myself about Arab ways of
tending a baby. Finally, however, the baby made it clear that
it was his supper time, and it was ours too. Again we

departed with friendly "Ma'a salamehs" singing in our ears
as we made our way back to our own supper table.

3. An Old City Courtyard

Just before Easter, Labiba, a Greek Orthodox maid at the
school, invited me to go shopping with her for material for
new aprons. With her, I had a chance to enter one of the
inviting courts in the Old City of Jerusalem that I had only
glimpsed through narrow doors in the stone walls that make
the medieval city a maze. The model city built for the
Montreal Exposition is the nearest thing in North America to
old Jerusalem where houses are heaped one beside, one atop
another in what seems slum crowding and confusion to an
outsider. The end result is much the same as "Habitat
"67",which took old Mediterranean cities as its inspiration.
Each tiny living area has its own small court paved with
time-polished stone, perhaps on a roof of another house,
perhaps at street level. The most amazing thing about these
stacks of houses is that almost every window has both
privacy and a vista.

With Labiba I went first to the yard-goods shop and then to
the dress-maker's home. The young seamstress was
Labiba's friend and she happily led me through a gate in a
stone wall into a court yard, up a flight of stone steps with
an iron-grill railing,into another court on top of a roof, and
finally up four more steps into her house. Here we were
served some delicious liqueur (Muslims almost always serve

coffee, Christians often serve spirits in Jordan), and Greek pastries. They were light and rich and just right after our rather long walk through the twisting cobblestone city streets. After we had eaten, the seamstress measured Labiba and we all chatted in a collage of languages about Easter, painted eggs, and where the girls were working. Then it was time for me to make my way back down into the suq with its tantalizing odors of roasting nuts and steaming coffee and sizzling sweets, its many-colored strings of shoes and beads, its sheep carcasses hanging over the stare-eyed heads draining into pans, its scarves, its copper, its antiquities. I ran down steps and up steps and through narrow alleys, and arrived outside the great, shadowy Damascus Gate just in time to make the five-minute walk to the school for the supper hour.

The walled city, Labiba's home, was a wonderful place. Princeton streets, where we walk now, seem dull by comparison. One evening some of the scholars from the school (with both husbands and wives) went to an old convent for dinner. Just as the sun went down we climbed some spiral stone steps to the roof. Off in the distance the dome of the Mosque of Omar glowed softly like a remembrance of the sun. Minarets pined the skyline, and on the narrow balcony of each there was a man, a muezzin. The evening crooned with his melancholy call to prayer,and the fawn-colored city lay hushed about us, windows shining with early evening lamps. For that moment there surely seemed to be but one God over all the town.

On summer evenings, when darkness had settled, when all
the shutters were pulled down over the shops, when
everyone was in his house, John and I used to go into the
Old City to watch the donkeys padding through quiet alleys
carrying great rocks for the restoration of the Church of the
Holy Sepulchre. It was eerie and suggestive to see the
noiseless beasts carrying their heavy burdens to the place of
the Cross.

4. Twins Are Born

Mohammad was Omar's assistant cook. Shortly after Easter
when we were all back at work, Mohammad's twins were
born. He came into the kitchen at noon, tired and a little
bent. My husband met him, and Mohammad told his
awesome news. He was father of two tiny boys. They had
been delivered at home by a midwife and Mohammad's
mother. Mohammad had, at first, been only delighted. This
young man, though, had never been a child, and his
responsibility for such a family fell upon him almost
immediately.

At the end of a week, I went to the kitchen where
Mohammad was cleaning up after breakfast. I puttered
about, wiped up a table, and then asked about the twins.
Mohammad always answers a question seriously. He
stopped what he was doing, looked directly at me, and said,
"I am worried. I don't know if they are well." When I asked
him what made him worry, he said, "Their eyes are yellow."

Since we had had a baby with anemia, this alerted me. I asked if he had called a doctor. He had, but the doctor was so busy he couldn't come to Mohammad's house for two days. I decided then, that I would try my own pediatricians. They, too, were so busy they could not go to the house, but each begged us to bring the babies to one of the two baby clinics. Mohammad said, "My wife and my mother, they are afraid. Arabs do not take their babies out when they are so little." I didn't like to impose my judgment on Mohammad's wife, but Mohammad himself was not at all sure of what to do. So I called one more Arab doctor we both knew who had been a pediatrician in Beirut. She was in bed with flu and was afraid of infecting the babies if she came, but she told me they should go to the hospital. "Arab women don't like to take them out," she said, "but tell him I said it will not hurt them, and they should see a doctor. Take them to Augusta Victoria. Dr. Khatibi is very good."

Since Dr. Khatibi had taken care of Pommy, I also knew he was very good. I explained all of this to Mohammad. He was, by this time, confident that this was the thing to do. One of the professors at the school was willing to drive to Mohammad's house in his Mercedes Benz, so we started off for Bethany once more. Mohammad lived even higher on the hill than Abu Mahmoud.

When we arrived I asked him to go ahead to tell his wife that we would take the babies to the hospital if she wished, but not to say she *must* take them just because we had come. He wanted us to come in immediately, however, and have coffee, disregarding the business at hand until the demands of hospitality had been fulfilled. When we went in, the women seemed to have been waiting for us. Mohammad must have had some sort of discussion with them before he left in the morning because he needed to explain very little. Apparently they had all decided they needed help.

This was a beautiful family. Mohammad was its head at 28. In 1948 the family had had to flee an Israeli invasion of his small town near Bethlehem. The father was sick. His mother had had almost to carry the sick man. The older sister carried the baby girl. Mohammad and his brother carried the only belongings they could save. Mohammad was sixteen when his father died. After that the family had a conference. They decided to educate one boy. Since his brother who was one or two years older than Mohammad already had a good beginning, Mohammad said he should go on to college. The younger brother then dropped out of school to support the family. He first became a cook and houseboy for a private family, then came to the American School where he cooked for the camps during archeological excavations and took Omar's place on Fridays, Omar's day off from the American School kitchen.

Mohammad's mother was a strong and intelligent woman. I have never met anyone who seemed to comprehend so well when a strange language was being spoken. She saw everything. Mohammad's wife was pretty, and as intelligent as his mother. These women wore their traditional Arab dress, as Abu Mahmoud's wife and mother had done, and it enhanced their dignity.

Until 1966, the family had lived in the refugee camp in
Jericho. In September of that year, the school felt it could
raise Mohammad's salary enough for him to rent a house
near Jerusalem. I was delighted. Before that Mohammad
had been able to go home only once a week. With his
brother in the University of Cairo, the family had had to be
very frugal since Mohammad's wage as an assistant cook
was a good bit less than Omar's.

When we went into the house, we did have one cup of
coffee. Mohammad's sister prepared it while the babies
were made ready for their outing. In the nursery, which was
the father's and mother's bedroom, there was only a double
bed pushed into a corner. The twins were swaddled and laid
crosswise in the middle of the bed. To let me see them,
Mohammad climbed onto the bed, and uncovered them. It
was like peering into a little rabbit's nest. There was a warm
kid-skin on top. Then a baby's blanket next to the babies.
Over their faces the mother had laid a very fine, clean scarf
to keep out the dust. They were so tiny they would have
been in an incubator had they been in the hospital.
Mahmoud, by this time weighed a bit over four pounds,
Ahmad weighed a bit less than four pounds.

These women had manufactured their own incubator with
the skins and blankets, and Mohammad kept a thermometer
in the room so when it became very cold he could light the
kerosene stove the school had given him. (I was again
grateful for John's generosity with the stoves.) I delighted in
the cleanness of this nursery room-- Palestinian houses
always seemed clean to me in the way that the desert and the

sky seem swept and scoured clean--but this room was so
immaculate I knew the twins were receiving the best of care.
I sipped my coffee while the twins were made ready for their
first outing, enjoying the hospitality that made me feel
welcome in all Palestinian homes.

After coffee, we started off. Mohammad carried Mahmoud.
His wife carried Ahmad. Mohammad's mother came too.
When we got to Augusta Victoria we had to climb three
flights of stone steps. It was a long climb for the new
mother and the old mother, and for me. But we did finally
arrive at the clinic on the top floor. When Dr.Khatibi was
free, he asked us to unwrap the babies and Mohammad
allowed me to take care of Mahmoud. I had never seen
swaddling before. The babies were simply wrapped tightly
in blankets and had fresh, much-washed, soft rags for
diapers. I was delighted to see no diaper rash. And so was
Dr. Khatibi. His examination proved that both babies were
in good health and were getting fine care. They needed
supplemental feeding, however, because two babies were
too much for Mohammad's wife to nurse without help.

Mohammad smiled,"I am glad we went," he said. "All of the
women of the village were telling us to give them first one
thing and then another. It is better to ask a doctor." I
remembered all the old wives' advice I had received when I
was a young mother in Princeton, New Jersey.

We took the babies back to the clinic the next month. I tried
to pay Dr. Khatibi but he would take nothing. Like all Arab

businessmen we encountered, he was a good businessman,
but also extremely generous both with himself and his gifts.

5. Issawiya, A Village in the Shadow of Mt. Scopus

Finally in early May we went to Qassim's house. Qassim
was older and the most bashful of all the school's staff. I
finally asked him if we could come. On the arranged
afternoon we started out, with all of our family *and* Qassim
once more in the Volkswagon. This trip was an adventure.
Qassim lived in Issawiya, a tiny village on the far side of Mt.
Scopus. The road to the village led through territory
restricted by the Israelis . One could not use the road at all
after sundown. Qassim, therefore, boarded at the school
and joined his family only on his day off. We looked for a
house for him all year, but since he owned the one in his
village and had some income from an olive grove on his
land, he could not bring himself to give it up.

We came to the Israeli outpost and Qassim had to show his
pass. We showed our passports and explained why we
wanted to go through. The guard was kind, but the
experience was unnerving. When he waved us on we
twisted along the pot-holed road under the shadow of Mt.
Scopus which loomed over us like a fortress. Every few
yards we passed a pill box. I shall never forget how the little
hairs on the back of my neck stiffened when I realized that it
was a woman who peered out of one of them, training her
gun on us. Although I can't explain why, a woman behind a

gun seems far more sinister than a man. I had never
contemplated a woman bearing arms before that encounter.

Qassim's house lay in a fold of the mountain. The
mountain, curling like an exotic and frightening serpent
around the village, is the most beautiful in the area. From
the Jerusalem side one is aware only of its height and
desolation. From Qassim's side it seemed almost
voluptuous with groves of evergreen the Israelis irrigated
with scarce and precious water. Arabs almost always raise
fruit-bearing trees.

Children played and laughed outside Qassim's Issawiah
cottage, and inside, the table was gaily spread with a
checked tablecloth and his wife's freshly baked cake and
coffee. We spent a happy hour. While his twelve-year old
boy visited with us easily in English, even the younger
children tried a few English words that they had learned in
the public school in the village. We were familiar with the
public schools since there was one next to the American
School, and our children used to sit on the wall watching
longingly the children playing games and celebrating special
festivals. In twenty years, the Jordanian school system had
been extended greatly. Bedouins had built new villages and
when they settled for the winter, even the tribal children
went to the village schools. When, in summer, the Bedouin
travelled, we often saw their children sitting in a circle on the
ground, notebooks in hand listening intently to the teacher.
Much of the learning was rote, but new and revolutionary
ideas were born in schools as they have been since schools
began.

In the shadow of the mountain, however, we all kept an eye
on our watches. Our visit was a short one, and much as we
enjoyed it, we were relieved to get back to our car, wave
goodbye to all the village children, pass as inconspicuously
as possible under those pillboxes once more, and finally
emerge at the guard house. Once the Arabs had tried to pave
this miserable road but their work was blown up in the
night. We knew the fields were mined because every once
in a while we heard reports of an accident when someone
strayed into them. In springtime it is hard to remember that a
flower-matted field can be dangerous, and there are no
fences to mark the forbidden areas.

6. Ramallah

In the little city of Ramallah it was even harder than it was in
Bethany or Issawiya to remember that peace was precarious.
The American Friends' School which so many American
children attended seemed imperturbable. Going to Ramallah
was, to us, like going home,though on the way, we passed
the place in the road where we could see Israeli cars heading
for the Mediterranian beaches where so many of our
Palestinian friends swam in the hot summers before 1948.

As they had as children, the families of three of our
colleagues at Princeton lived in this town high on the brim of
the lush valley of Samaria. The spring grasses reminded me
of the succulent waster cress I gathered by the mill pond

when I was a child, and it was in this valley in April that our
children gathered armloads of anemones. When we visited
the Ramallah homes of lawyers, businessmen, and doctors,
we spoke not only in our own language but in our own
patterns of thought and were thoroughly understood. After
desert and coffee, and, always, Janin oranges, we talked, as
we do at home, of ethics and morality, of peace and justice
and goodness and complexity, with the Mikhails, the
Melikians, the Ziadehs, the Shehadis. Their homes seemed
deep with generosity, gentleness, and the warmth of love.

III.

June: The Six Day War

But our memories always turn eventually to the end of
spring, to Monday, June 5. It was a beautiful sunny day.
We were left at the American School with only one other
professor. Everyone else had gone, but we were awaiting
John's successor who was due at any moment. The air was
charged with foreboding, but, since our term was to end
July 1, we hoped to turn the affairs of the school over to him
in orderly fashion. For about a week before the eruption of
shooting, everyone in the city was nervous.

On Friday I was in the dining room working with
Mohammad. I asked, "Mohammad, do you think we should
go?" He looked at me very soberly, "I think you should
go." Unaccountably, I was hurt by his answer. "Why?" I

asked. "Because", he said, "your ships are coming to attack our country." What the "Liberty" was doing, no one then knew. A Syrian friend of mine speculated that the American ship perhaps jammed the Egyptian radar communications the morning of the Israeli surprise attack. I was too tense to allow for Mohammad's revelation.

For days, a constant flow of raucous Arabic had been coming from the transistor radios in the kitchen as if the din of rams' horns and shouting could tumble the wall and the Mandelbaum Gate.

Since I knew that the reconnaissance planes we had watched drift over East Jerusalem all year, had told, already, precisely everything that was on our side of the wall, the noise set my teeth on edge. I grew defensive at the accusation. As I warmed to my subject, I covered the whole area of propaganda and repressed news, the weakness of the Arab forces, and the inefficiency and bureaucracy of Middle East culture. My fears for him, for all of our Palestinian friends and for my own family made my voice harsh. Mohammad listened quietly and intently. At the end he asked me gently what I wanted him to do in the upstairs apartment.

Saturday night we couldn't sleep. All night we could hear heavy wheels growling on the Israeli side of the "Wall". The Mandelbaum Gate was only two blocks from the school. John recognized the implacable rumble of tanks. I had never heard them before.

Sunday morning we went to church and in the afternoon, Lizzie Nasser and some of our other Arab friends stopped by for tea. Unfortunately, I think they were reassured to find us still there. Americans,we would surely know the worst and get our children to safety. I think they didn't believe our ignorance. But even though Evan Wilson the American Consul , had repeatedly called all of the Americans left in the city together to the consulate where we pooled our information, we all remained innocent of Israel's plans.

The news on Monday morning was good. Nasser was to go to America to discuss the "situation". Mohammad came to me at breakfast. "You should stay now", he said. I was overjoyed. We finished breakfast and walked to the post office. On the way, we met our taxi driver who had been drafted into the Jordanian Army two weeks before. He was in civilian clothes and home awaiting further orders. The city was relaxed. Shops were open and young Mr. Melikian in the yarn import shop (his father having died, the family says "mercifully", in the month before) pointed out on his map an area from Bethlehem to Nazareth which could become a religious enclave governed by the United Nations. Around the corner, Ohan, the antiquities dealer, had marked out a slightly smaller area on his map. We returned to the school to take the children to visit the Mosque of Omar and the Pool of Siloam.

But inside the American School door we met Omar with a radio in his hand. Mohammad and Mahmoud, their kaffias drawn like shrouds around their faces, stood stiff and pale

beside him. "It has started," he said. "What has started?"
John asked. "The troubles in Egypt," Omar told him.

We knew exactly what we had to do. The children and I
finished packing and I began catching up last minute odds
and ends. John, my husband, went to take care of the office
details, to officially turn the school over to Omar until our
replacement arrived, and leave as much order as he could. I
hurried Mohammad, Mahmoud, Kassim and Labiba off to
go to their families and hailed a ride "out" for a young
woman anthropologist who had remained in the city to finish
a project. Her rescuer was an old timer at the British School
for Archeology, and I was sure the leathery "Brit's" long
experience in the deserts of the Middle East would stand
both him, an archeological architect ,and the novice
anthropologist in good stead. Together, they headed straight
"out" for Damascus and Lebanon.

At eleven twenty, we bade Omar goodbye, telling him to go
to his family. I knew his wife had been having dizzy spells
all week because of the tension. Standing by the taxi he had
called for us, he pointed out a huge cannon which had just
been raised to the top of the Italian Hospital on the "other
side". Its muzzle was directed straight at our door. I
shuddered and went to the car. The children were quarreling
about who should sit by the window. Where Omar found
that taxi I shall never know, for by this time the streets were
empty, the shops closed, the shutters all rolled down. John
and Professor Horne were to sit in front. The three children
and I were to sit in back. We had all of our luggage and all

of Professor Horne's with us in that car. The children did have something to fuss about.

As I tried to push Fleur over, the first gun fired from directly behind me. It had to be from Mt. Scopus. Omar said, "Hurry!" and ran inside. Professor Horne shut my door and climbed in front. As we drove through the school gate, he said, "It is eleven-twenty-five." I don't know why the hour seemed so portentous.

War spread over the city as if that first lone shot had set afire a sheet of gasoline. When we got around the corner, several Arabs were setting up a machine gun in front of the radio station. At the museum we were caught in crossfire between Israeli guns on Mt. Scopus and Arab guns in the museum's fortress-like tower. Our children put their heads down, but not before the face of a woman carrying a bag with a loaf of bread sticking out from its bulge, was etched on their memories. Tears ran down her cheeks and a bullet ricocheted off the street, just missing her.

Our driver sped on. As we came under the Mount of Olives near Bethany he pulled into a gas station, but the station was out of gas. Pulling out, we were again in crossfire between Israeli guns from the Church of the Dormition and Arab guns from the garden at the top of the Mount of Olives near Augusta Victoria. Ahead a bus was blocking the road. People were piling out of it like bags of grain humping into a ditch. Our driver whipped into a side road skimming higher along the Mountain where he dove between houses for shelter. We came onto the main road again, just as the

Church of the Dormition on the other side of "no man's land" blew up, the dome opening like a slow motion picture of a flower unfolding, telling us that Israeli munitions had been stored there. It was, we were told later, just at that moment that Ted Yates, a U.S. reporter, was killed immediately above us at the Intercontinental Hotel on the crest of the storied mountain we were circling.

On the side of this mountain, the houses of Omar, Mohammad, and Abu Mahmoud all hung like stalled ducks at a shooting gallery. Our driver raced on, and finally we were out of the firing, careening down the winding pass to the Jordan River.

There on the plain at the foot of the pass, all of the Jordanian artillery, tanks, half tracks, trucks, were arranged on a neat grid like stars on a flag of truce. We sped across the Allenby Bridge and on… up to the Amman Airport. From the back seat I remember saying weakly, "If I were an Israeli, I'd bomb the airport first." But the men thought we might find passage on some last plane out. When we got to the gate, however, the Arab flight attendants obviously agreed with me. Piled into a jeep, they were heading fast away from the landing strip. So, turning around, we headed for the American Embassy, well imagining how pleased they would be to see us.

(Post Script 1993: April Glasby was then at the Amman desk routing all refugees to the safe house chosen by the embassy.)

Finally, we reached shelter at another Intercontinental Hotel on the outskirts of Amman where all Western evacuees were gathered for the next six days. We pulled under the portico just in time to dash to the air raid shelter, leaving our bags in the car, before Israeli planes did bomb the Amman Airport. Great black clouds rolled up from the wreckage of oil tanks for several days afterward.

During the next three nights we had little sleep because air raid sirens kept driving us back to the shelter. All the while we could see the flashes of fire and hear the shelling of our beloved Jerusalem. The Arab waiters and servants were as gracious as though we were guests in their homes, but as they served us, tears hung in their eyes, eyes which ferreted out goodies for our children even when the food ran low.

Their kindness seemed the greater when we realized that they were convinced that American planes were helping Israel. One man who had been strafed on the road down to the Jordan from Jerusalem told us that the attacking plane bore U.S. insignia. In the air raid shelter one night, I asked the woman sitting next to me what was being said in Arabic on the radio her husband and children gathered around. She told me with the same straight look that I had come to respect in Mohammad, "They say American planes are bombing us." We were unsure even after Mr. Findley Burns, our ambassador, published a statement saying he could guarantee that no American planes or soldiers were aiding the attack.

On Saturday, all of us who had lived together for a week as if we were aboard a phantom ship, were evacuated in the most efficient and sympathetic operation I can imagine. The bombing of the airport had made our evacuation a complicated puzzle. There were many reasons for getting us out soon. Food was running low, Amman's water supply was being strained to its limit, and returning defeated soldiers added an explosive element to the crowded city.

The American and British embassy personnel showed the sensitivity to the situation that makes us, even now, very grateful.

Having received instructions, one by one in our rooms at about ten o'clock the night before, at four o'clock in the morning, we, the evacuees, began congregating noiselessly in the hotel lobby.

Our family bid an admiring and appreciative adieu to Mr. Dana Adams Schmidt of the *New York Times* . He had decided to remain behind because he "was getting out a story a day", and he thought someone should be in Amman from his paper. Throughout the whole week he had shown an understanding of Arab ways and Arab humiliation which we saw was unusual with reporters trying to get uncensored news. Mr. Schmidt knew how to drink coffee and listen without being angered by the difficulties reporters encountered in the mounting tension.

Then, as we were assigned because of the children, we got into the first car, and slowly, silently, a cavalcade of private

cars and taxi cabs slipped out onto the road like a ship
departing from its dock. It floated all around the
outskirts of the city, still silently, silently, past silent details
of Jordanian soldiers stationed at each crossroad to guard us
on our way. At the airport, when we arrived, baggage which
had been sent ahead by truck was set out alphabetically. As
each car drew up, the passengers, quickly and still with little
talking, gathered their baggage and went to their assigned
departure stations.

A half-hour later, the first plane, a great whale of an army
transport with hot breath and an enormous gut to suck up
passengers, took off, loaded with nearly one-hundred
mothers, fathers, and children. Within a half hour another
plane lifted off, and another and another until all of the
nearly one-thousand people stranded at the hotel with us or
around the city, were carried away…to Teheran where, once
more, American Embassy people took care of us with hotel
reservations, hot dogs and hamburgers and baked beans,
and currency exchanges… and, finally, flights to Europe.

It was a heartbreaking way to end our delightful year in
Jordan, a year in which hospitality, Arab and, at the end,
American, had graced our days.

On April 25, 1968, ten months later, Miss Halaby, having
once more rejuvenated her house after Israeli troops were
billeted there, is in jail.

Because their houses were in the immediate line of fire,
Omar's family, and Mohammad and Mahmoud with their

families, fled through back wadis to the Jericho oasis. As
Mohammad was walking back up the mountain to see if his
house and his belongings had survived the shelling, he was
arrested by Israeli troops, forced to get into a truck, and
transported to the Amman side of the Jordan River. His
family was sent over shortly afterwards. Although he and
American friends have tried to get permission for him to
return to the home he so newly acquired, he was not allowed
back into Jerusalem then or until now, since he fell into all
the categories the Israelis fear: he was younger than thirty
years old, he lived in Jerusalem itself, and he was a refugee
in 1948. Abu Mahmoud smuggled himself back in the trunk
of a friend's car. His family returned later. Omar's family,
too, is once more back home.

We were on one side of the wall. On the other side
American friends, who were spending the year there, were
experiencing many of the same fears and tensions we were.
Often last year the modern East and West seemed as far apart
as Kipling's. Israel is a Western culture, with Western
purpose and a Western sense of nation. The Jordan River is
only a muddy creek, but where it divides Israelis from
Palestinians, the gulch is wide and deep. Even words are
used to different ends. Symbols, music, formal patterns of
speech are the means of Eastern communication. The
logical, analytical statement used in the West seems self-
serving, powdery, contrived, and impertinent to the Oriental
mind.

All of the problems contemporary societies meet existing
together in one world must be faced in the Middle East.

Justice, love, even a homeland, are too intangible, too
delicate to be conceived in war. War only creates exiles who
crowd some neighboring country, rubbing their new
homeland raw and sore and explosive. We scarcely dare to
hope that the people of the Near East will ever cross the
gulch to meet each other as Jacob and the angel did,
wrestling together until morning comes, until they find
peace.

Post Script: October, 1993

When the American Schools for Oriental Research opened a center in Amman after the '67 war, Mohammad became cook. He is still there. The twins are 27 years old, the two eldest of six children.

When Augusta Victoria Hospital was set afire by Israeli shells, Dr. Majaj and Dr. Khatibi were nearly trapped in the basement. Shown an exit by a dear friend, they ran on foot down the back of the Mount of Olives to safety. Dr. Majaj returned later, and is still taking care of his people, though he seldom plays his violin these days.

John Mikail left teaching at Princeton University in 1968 to join the PLO, feeling he could no longer remain aloof from his people's misery. He was killed, it has been reported, on a ship which sank on its way from Beirut to Tripoli. His cousin, Hanan Ashrawri carries on his work for peace.

The elder Melikians, Armenian refugees who found a home in Jordan, are dead. Two of the younger Melikians, after living many years in Beirut where Levon taught at the American University, moved twice more, first to Qatar where Levon taught psychology for several years, and now, with no place in the Middle East to call home anymore, to Toronto. All of their surviving family is now in Canada. Asia and Sophie Halaby are still living in the same house, entirely disillusioned with the Americans they trusted. Refugees from Russia at the beginning of their lives, now at the end of their lives, they live, still,in the land which gave them shelter, in a land of shattered dreams. They don't march anymore. They've learned that an army can take over your house at any time, even in a democracy.

Now, in 1993, Palestinians and Israelis have reawakened once more, their search for peace. We dare faint hope, our breath baited.

THE RONDANINI PIETA
Michaelangelo's Offering: Their Very Bodies
(as though they do not belong only to him)

Michaelangelo, at last,
Knocked off even the Head
The virgin lifted,
Hacked all polish off,
Let light whack its contra dictions.
He chiseled, out of the Woman's bosom,
The buoyant Head of Man,
His legs a-dangle,
No longer needed to bear His weight,
No longer needed to bear Her weight,
Her Head a flux of His.
Two loves ...Love
Lifting into the Father.
Jutting angles relaxed,
Embrace becomes a yoke,
We, a light load.
Their spiring
      earthen
         Love
Dumbfounds. Becomes.

Michaelangelo
Rondanini Pieta
Milan
Castello Sforzesco

SCAPEGOATS, LAMBS, AND DOVES

This human comedy is dedicated especially to Wadiah who made our lives so pleasant at The American School in 1959 - 60. Her savory meals, her impeccable ironing, her polishing our floors, her accounts of happenings in her village, the folk stories she retold as the old woman in her village had told them to her made our lives in a strange land with three small children wonderfully comfortable. But it was Wadiah's loving care of our baby that most endeared her to us.

Wadiah was a single woman who lived with her extended family in Beit Jallah near Bethlehem. A devout Greek Orthodox Christian, she introduced us to many of the rites of the Orthodox Church, and, in January, took us to a baptism of infants in the Jordan River . That experience became the story of "Scapegoats, Lambs, and Doves" , a dramatic poem that centers around Wadiah, that celebrates the doggedness of her faith, faith that lets her live easily with contradiction : with free will and predestination, with chance and necessity, hearing foreign tongues in her own language.

I have fictionalized and dramatized the event, trying to see why the story of that baptism, the happening itself and the piety of the participants made me more sympathetic to the many forms of fundamentalism in the Middle East . A modern American trained in "scientific method" I am shocked by sacrifice, by tales of the immolation of whole battalions of child-soldiers sent out as vanguards, and by terrorism, self-sacrificial terrorism in the name of God.

*These horrors, however, have seemed to be answers for
many of those who find themselves to be the sacrificial lamb
on the world's altar, for those confronted with the slogan
"A land without a people for a people without a land",
confronted with the unheeding deletion of their ancient and
established communities.*

*As a sacrificed people, Palestinians have been forced to ask
what God requires of them. They vigorously reject being
made the scapegoat for the world's injustice, and at the same
time, they struggle to please a Creator so unfathomable and
unpredictable as theirs by further sacrificing themselves.
Knowing such contradiction to be the stuff of true religion,
I pondered Wadiah and the Baptism.*

*Wadiah, one of the dispossessed Palestinian women, is full
of grace. She lives face to face with the demands of her
own scripture, with the sign of the cross, with the metaphor
of baptism (being buried with Christ and risen with Him) .
Though she asks "Who knows the mind of the Lord" , she is
never deaf to Paul's exhortation, "Present your very selves
to him: a living sacrifice..."*

*The demands her faith made on her at the baptism of her
nephew in the Jordan River also made me wonder what
demands such faith may make on God. So I established
contradicting voices as I wrote. Some of the radical
"fundamentalists" , many of the young dispossessed former
inhabitants of "the land without a people" seem driven to
prayer and "acts of devotion " that often appear to outsiders
to be bargaining with God, though in any of the three Middle*

*Eastern religions, a quid pro quo with God is blasphemy.
Others of the dispossessed blaspheme bitterly against all
religion. Driving a people to blasphemy must be the worst of
blasphemies. But it may be our secularist capitalist eyes that
cause us to see only the hope of a bargain in an act of
sacrifice.It is hard for us to believe that any act is sacred.
Americans like to solve problems with a down-to-earth-
"positive" method. Overwhelmingly appalled at Hitler's
exterminating the Jews, they thought that by establishing
Israel they had brought some justice to the victims of the
Holocaust. But far from Judah and Samaria, we turned a
blind eye to a second injustice, the quiet erasure of
Palestinians from the country they had lived in for
thousands of years. I suppose my own guilt in this
scapegoating made me unusually susceptible to the
symbolism of this sacrament at the Jordan River.*

*As I thought about the dramatic baptism I watched, it
became, in my eyes, a sacrifice: The boat figured the altar;
the water, fire; the baby, the lamb; the dove, Godot; and
the expatriot, the scapegoat snagged in the bush, homeless.*

*Thinking about the "bloodiness" of the event, conscious that
 "The good that I would, I do not, … the evil I would not, I
do…" the question became , not only : Why do we meddle
and try to right wrong? The question became: How can
there be any place in a scientific world for the hallowed act?
Why do any of us partake of Christian sacraments?*

*This story is about Wadiah's faith. She faced the intractable
poverty of her beloved family with hard, hard work, with*

119

selfless generosity, with unquenchable gusto for life, with sacrificial love.Wadiah brought us many gifts , gifts of care and embroidery and story, but mostly, wrenching gifts of spirit. Believing in her heart, even in a land where, to create justice, injustice was created, that "a little child shall lead" us all, she lets that happen as best she can.

Readings: from the King James Version of the Bible:
Matt.3:1-6, Mark 1:-11, Luke 3: 1-18, Is. 35, Is. 55, Is. 12,
I Cor. 10: 1-4, Romans 6, Matt. 28:19-20.

SCAPEGOATS, LAMBS AND DOVES

Characters: Wadiah:

>Dresses in a simple, western-style, cotton housedress with a sweater pulled about her. She is a large-boned village woman, independent, intelligent,motherly . Her speeches, delivered with her head held proudly high,are somewhat defiant, like shafts sent into an unremitting sun. Her bosom is soft and her bearing is kind.

Said: (boy sitting on the top of the ladder at right downstage)

>a very young man, wiry, strong,."out-of-it"…Unable to reconcile the injustice of his world with Wadiah's faith. Wearing a western sweater and trousers, he wraps a checked kufiyya on his head. Said lives in the old city of Jerusalem. As with most of the young men in Palestine, he cannot find work. He holds a pad and pencil.

Rifaat: (boy caught in the thorn bush. He sits on the top of the left ladder)

>rounder, somewhat glum . He wears western clothes. Rifaat, Said's cousin, is a university student in Soviet-governed Prague (1960), an expatriot, bitter at the fate of his country. He is also "out"

The Bishop:

>A *very* round fellow with a

beard and hair pulled into a short
pony tail. He wears the mantle and vestments
of a Greek Orthodox Bishop.
3 priests:
Dress much like the bishop.
Bishop and priests wear appropriate
hats.
Mona: Wadiah's niece,
Wears a simple western cotton housedress,
and sweater that is too thin. She is rather
shy, but also a bit independent, certainly
intelligent and kind.
Ramon: (Mona's husband)
wears western
trousers and shirt with a kafia.
He is emaciated and has
worked too hard. His jacket is
threadbare..
Majed: (their baby)
about a year or 14 months old. Dressed in a
loose, brown wrap.
American man:
an American liberal, dresses in casual
clothes, with a sweater. Kind, tall, a bit
intellectual, open-minded.
American woman:
a peahen, also an
American liberal do-gooder,
concerned, dresses sensibly but in a
designer sweater

Maid:
> Dresses in Jerusalem traditional dress
> (black, embroidered) with white tarhah
> covering her hair. She is young and pretty.
> and good with babies.

Crowd:
> Some dress in Arab, some in
> western clothes, a few more Arab
> than western. Sweaters and shawls
> cover arms and heads. All are in a
> holiday mood.

Vendor:
> Carrying bread in a basket on his
> head, he wears Turkish trousers, a
> shirt, and a thread-bare jacket.

Bell-ringer:
> Woman in white, embroidered in
> blue, Ramallah dress with a tarhah
> covering her hair.

Setting:
> Running down the center of the stage, and
> toward us, is the Jordan River, at the sight where
> Jesus was baptized. There is an old scow anchored
> at center stage, its prow toward the audience. On the
> bank, only slightly to right, is a small lectern. At far
> right downstage slightly is a step ladder four feet
> high . There is a cache of small rocks at the foot of
> the ladder. Upstage at left, across the river, a step-
> ladder, six or eight feet high, or higher, almost in a
> thorn tree that branches over it.

On the apron downstage extreme left stands an
ironing board with a shirt on it, and an iron. At
right, the apron is a sunny field which stretches from
the river, and spreads downstage. One or two large
rocks lie about. Steps lead to the field accessible
from the center aisle. There is a bit of green here, but
it is very spare.The sky is blue-blue and it is warm
here near the Dead Sea: People wear sweaters and
shawls but loosen them.

Time:

About 10:00 a.m. the day of the celebration of
Epiphany, part of the Festival of Light. The Christian
festival celebrates the manifestation of the divine
nature of Christ to the Gentiles. On this feast day, it
is the tradition of the Greek Orthodox Church in
Palestine to celebrate the sacrament of Baptism at the
sight where Jesus was baptized.
The story of the Three Magi from distant lands is
said to be a story figuring God's revelaton of
Himself in Christ. So Wadiah speaks of their
bringing gifts on the Twelfth Day of Christmas.

This all takes place in January, 1960.

As the curtain rises:

Rifaat sits on the top of the right ladder, caught in the
thornbush.Throughout, he works periodically to
untangle himself. He has a clipboard and pencil
beside him. Said sits on the other ladder with a pad
on his knee, pencil in hand. A loaf of bread is beside
him which he picks at periodically. A crowd is

126

gathering from all sides on both the left and right
shores of the river. Everyone carries a lunch either
in a basket or wrapped in a kufiyya; children munch
oranges and sweets. Many women carry both babies
and lunch baskets. A woman, the bell-ringer, stands
on a chair in the balcony (wherever it is in the
auditorium) (maybe on a ladder at the back of an
aisle) vigorously pulling the rope of a tinny-sounding
bell. Wadiah, Mona carrying Majed, and Ramon
stand by the bell ringer, wherever she is. As the bell
begins to ring Wadiah tucks the baby's blanket
around him and begins to hurry them all. She is
obviously excited, and so fleet the others can hardly
keep up with her as they come down from the
balcony into the rear of the side aisle and hesitate.
They will finally follow the bishop's procession
down another aisle. In the bishop's aisle at the back,
the procession, (the Bishop, three priests, and two
soldiers) lines up, balancing all the accoutrements for
the baptismal ceremony: stoles, pulpit Bible, large
prayerbook, flowers, staff, a Cross on a standard, a
bowl for oil, a jar of oil, and a second small alabaster
or silver, vial of oil that the Bishop may tuck into his
robe, etc. There is a county fair feeling and a county
fair odor of meat patties, fried cakes and gazooze
(soda).Wadiah, Mona and her baby, and Ramon will
follow at the rear of this procession.

Said: (Beginning to write- right to left- while the procession
comes on, munching the Arab bread...)
    My dear Rifaat,

Hear it.
Ding, ding, dang! Ding ting, ting, dang!
The bishop's charwoman, poised to fly
Clinks her bells on a blue tin sky.
And Wadiah pushes Mona down the stair.
I'd bet she'll dare set her
Right on the train of the bishop's gown!
Mona can always trust Wadiah.
She scrubs and polishes
Even begs, slyly of course,
Out there at the American School
To get some sentimental soul
(I am kind today, I said "soul")
To give some little gift
To her brother or sisters,
Because of the "troubles".
Someone *is* sending Irfan to school.
Backed into the corners of all
The Jerusalem walls,
She acts as though Wilson's Arch,
Buried there under the Wailing Wall,
Is a rainbow she can unearth.
She's determined to placate the God
Of Abraham, Isaac and Jacob, Ishmael,
Mohammad, AND
Her own Little Lord Jesus!

By this time the procession is coming down the aisle. On
stage people mill about near the lectum, pushing the boat in
and out in anticipation and causing a lot of nervous action.
American wife: (on stage at the right side of the river)

See, That's just like the dress
I bought from Wadiah! Not so clean,
And the embroidery isn't as fine.
I suspect Wadiah's aunt made my dress
For her own wedding, and then became
That girl who "did something wrong".

Said: (Still writing)
Why, she's even begged for you, my friend.
One family from the school is flying back
By way of Austria.You'll get a letter soon
Suggesting that you risk your neck
Slipping over the Czech border
To meet them in Vienna.
They'll take you home on a rug
To America if you wish.
I don't know why
Wadiah thinks these Americans
Can help you, me, Mona or the baby.
They'll be like all the others.
They'll go back to the U.S.
And they'll have to be careful there
Not to be "anti-Semitic"!
Anti-Semitic! Who is a Semite?!

American wife:
Wadiah wants us to come out to Beitjallah.
She has a letter from Rifaat.

Said:

I don't suppose you want to go with them.
You've had the courage
To make your own breaks.
Once in a while I'm sick to death
Of tea and rice cakes…
And I wish I could join you, or go to Cairo.
Home's a tighter trap than ever.
No jobs
But carrying packages
Or directing tours through our "holy city"
For "baksheesh'.

American wife: (as the vendor passes selling vials of
distilled water, Jordan water.)
Maybe we should buy some.
It might be nice to use
In the font back home.
I'm so glad we left Robert
At the school.…all this trachoma!
Wadiah said she wished
We'd have Robert
Baptized with Majed. Ugh!

Said:
Ha!
It takes someone like Wadiah!
Here she is now
Bribing God.
For some favor for Mona
Or Majed.
Here they come.

Sure enough,
Mona's right behind
The bishop,
Leading the procession
Of the worthy.

Wadiah: (As they come down the aisle)
        When the water's blessed, it's sweet.

Mona:
        And deep!

Wadiah:
        Jesus loves this spot

Mona:
        The water's dark

Wadiah:
        This is the day of the Magi

Mona:
        They didn't come to my baby

Wadiah:
        Jesus likes all babies. They are pure

Mona:
        Then why should Majed be baptized?!

Wadiah:

The magi brought God gifts. And they were wise.

Mona:

Suppose he dies…

Said:

Wadiah's brave. She'll risk anything,
Even Majed!
Mona, she's still a child.
She trusts Wadiah
To find a way.
Ramon's sickness is getting worse.
He's spitting blood now
And he can hardly lift
Even small rocks into place any more.
I could get a job over there
Where he works. What for?
Pile one rock on another?
And they never fit.
Nothing's done right,
Nothing's plumb here.

The procession comes up on the stage, still balancing all the paraphernalia. The Americans go to Wadiah, Mona and Ramon.

American woman:

Hello, Mona!
Wadiah said you'd have Majed.
(takes baby's finger)

Aren't you proud of him, Ramon?
I've knit a new blanket for him
To wear at his baptism.
(She gives the wrapped gift to Mona)

Wadiah: (taking the gift to hold it for Mona)
   A baby's naked when he's baptized.
But, after…in the field,
This will warm him…
With the sun.

Said:

This whole Holy Land's
In a pretty plight!
But Wadiah goes ahead
Scheming for favors
From
The American,
From the sun,
From this God of hers…

Ramon: (going aside and sitting on the ground with his head
in his hands)
(He spits.)
What more can be done?
I'm worse than Job. I *am* dung,
Christian spitting blood
Wadiah goes to Ramon.

Ramon:

In a city where the Church is a sepulchre,

The wall a wailing wall,
And the only sun that rises out of the walls
To proclaim to all who approach
"This is the Holy City",
Is the gold dome of the mosque!
Layers of walls dug up.
Layers of conquerors.
Layers of hate.
Layers of helplessness.
Layers of dung heaps.

Wadiah:
   A lamb must be pure.
   This is the Festival of Light.
   A blessing's sure.

Ramon:
   What does God want of Me?

Wadiah:
   You've loved mercy,
   You've done justice,
   You've walked humbly

Said:
   God knows, he's walked humbly,
   …Walked numbly.

Wadiah:
   Now you must sacrifice.

Said:

>Sacrifice!

Wadiah:(pointing to a young leafless tree at the edge of the river near the boat -- It looks like a cross.)

>See, the forked stick!

Ramon:

>To hang him.

The bishop and priests finally arrange themselves about the lectern..Wadiah has pushed and maneuvered and bullied and cajoled the way for Mona, Ramon, Majed, and the Americans to go to the front. The bishop takes his place at the lectern, two priests hold another large Bible for a third to read. There is a general din, and the priests don't have hands enough to hold the Bible, the Cross, the flowers, and the oil. The people continue to mill about until the moment of Baptism.

Bishop:

>THE READING OF THE HOURS:
>The Gospel of Jesus Christ, the Son Of God:

First Priest:

>The word of God came unto John the son of
>Zacharias in the wilderness. And he came unto all
>the country about Jordan, preaching the baptism of
>repentance for the remission of sins; As it is written

in the book of the words of Esaias the prophet,
saying,

> The voice of one cryng in the wilderness,
> Prepare ye the way of the Lord,
> Make his paths straight.
> Every valley shall be filled,
> > And every mountain and hill shall be
> > brought low;
> And the crooked shall be made straight,
> And the rough ways shall be made smooth;
> And all flesh shall see the salvation of God.

Then said he to the multitude that came forth to be
baptized of him, O generation of vipers, who hath
warned you to flee from the wrath to come? Bring
forth therefore fruits worthy of repentance, and begin
not to say within yourselves, We have Abraham to
out father: for I say unto you, That God is able of
these stones to raise up children unto Abraham. And
now also the axe is laid unto the root of the trees:
every tree therefore which bringeth not forth good
fruit is hewn down, and cast into the fire.

And the people asked him, saying, What shall we do
then? He answereth and saith unto them, He that hath
two coats, let him impart to him that hath none; and
he that hath meat, let him do likewise. Then came
also publicans to be baptized, and said unto him,
Master, what shall we do? And he said unto them,
Exact no more than that which is appointed you.
And the soldiers likewise demanded of him, saying,
And what shall we do? And he said unto them, Do

violence to no man, neither accuse any falsely; and
be content with your wages. And as the people were
in expectation, and all men mused in their hearts of
John, whether he were the Christ, or not; John
answered, saying unto them all, I indeed baptize you
with water; but one mightier that I cometh, the latchet
of whose shoes I am not worthy to unloose: he shall
baptize you with the Holy Ghost and with fire:

Wadiah:
> Come up here. Listen.
> Now, listen.
> God wants a *living* sacrifice,
> Your whole self.
> You can't be afraid.

Second Priest:
> In those days came John the Baptist, preaching in the
> wilderness of Judea, And saying, Repent ye: for the
> kingdom of heaven is at hand. For this is he that
> was spoken of by the prophet Esaias, saying,
>> The voice of one crying in the wilderness,
>> Prepare ye the way of the Lord,
>> Make his paths straight.
> And the same John had his raiment of camel's hair,
> and a leathern girdle about his loins; and his meat
> was locusts and wild honey. Then went out to him
> Jerusalem, and all Judea, and all the region round
> about Jordan, and were baptized of him in Jordan,
> confessing their sins.

Wadiah:

> John baptized right here,
> Right down in that hollow
> By the boat. He stood out
> A little way in the water.

Third Priest:

> And it came to pass in those days, that Jesus came
> from Nazareth of Galilee and was baptized of John in
> Jordan.

Bishop:

> THE VOICE OF THE FATHER, THE DOVE OF
> THE SPIRIT, JESUS THE SON OF GOD:

Third priest:

> And straightway coming up out of the water, he saw
> the heavens opened, and the spirit like a dove
> descending upon him. And there came a voice from
> heaven, saying, "Thou art my beloved son, in whom
> I am well pleased."

Priests:

> Chant a Gloria

Wadiah:

> I was baptized here.
> I was a grown girl.
> You were only a baby then. (to Mona)
>
> It wasn't at Epiphany…
> But it was right here,

With all my family. Our old
Bishop took me out into the river.
He was strong.
Rifaat: (picking up his board and pen)
My dear Said,
How I enjoy word from you
I am alone too much.
I have run and run, as single-minded
As Wadiah, always a refugee.
Wadiah's latest idea,
This angel from America, comes too late.
I am prisoner in my own thorn bush.
School is cramped and rigid here.
I can't escape to Austria, or Jordan.
But does Wadiah really urge Mona
To have Majed baptized in the Jordan
At Epiphany? I was baptized there
In that charade.
You can see what it did for me!
In that pitiful muddy stream.
She's desperate.
She can't let go her dream of life…
In all that drought.
Running toward a wider river,
And some green, I shagged on a thorn.
She's right , though, Said.
Drown yourself there in the Jordan.
At best you'd hope a myth.
At worst, gasp some gallantry.
The Bishop and the priests have finished at the lectern and
now begin again to gather up the Bibles, Cross, flowers, oil,

and to move in some disarray through the crowd to the boat.
People keep reaching toward the Bishop who stops
periodically to bless them with the sign of the cross.

American woman:
> That boat looks a little precarious to me.
> How many help out in the ceremony?

Wadiah:
> The bishop does the baptism
> And the three priests read scripture
> And hold things for him
> While they are out there.

American woman:
> Do they do it right out in the boat
> On the river?

Wadiah:
> Not far from shore.

American woman:
> Does the bishop use water
> From the vendor
> Or does he prepare
> His own
> For the baptism?

Wadiah (with a kind of restrained ecstasy)
> What you mean?
> He puts the baby in the water,

In the river,
Head and all.
All bare
The baby drowns, and then he's reborn.
Pure.

American woman:
My God, Wadiah!
He'll put a fourteen month old baby
Into that water!?
It's cold! He'll get pneumonia…
If he doesn't get trachoma,
Or too much water in his lungs!

Wadiah :
He'll scream his lungs clear. (imperiously)

American woman:
That's pagan (in a pedantic voice)
God is Love.
God doesn't demand…

Wadiah:
Why does Ramon spit blood?
(tossing her head)
He loves his child.
He has to lift those rocks to feed his child.
Why else do you think he does it?
Ramon must sacrifice his first-born.

American woman:

But God! This is Jesus!

Wadiah:
    God made Ramon.
    He gave Ramon a baby without food.

American woman:
    Wadiah, you can't give the bishop
    This baby!
    The English gave you an education.
    You know the rules of sanitation.
    If Ramon's sick,
    You can't help the sick
    With a sacrifice…or magic!

Wadiah:
    Ramon is good.
    He goes to church every Sunday.
    He prays,
    He never hurt anyone.
    He never stole. He works as hard
    As he can.
    God doesn't hate him.
    He wants a gift from Ramon.

American woman:
    But not his baby, Wadiah!

Wadiah:
    Ramon has a pure heart.

He loves God.
God wants more from him.
He's not an American.
God wants a new lamb.
American woman:
Poor Mona. (moans it)

Wadiah:
Poor Hanna.Poor Sarah.
Poor Mary.

American woman:
Samuel just went to the temple.
And God sent a scapegoat
To Abraham.
Wadiah, Majed's blood will rot your skirt.

Wadiah:
It's God's.
The blood is God's.

Rifaat:
Crucified the Savior.
But God won.
They crucified the malefactor
And we hang beside him.
There's the retribution.
Poor Ramon.

The bishop and the priests and the two soldiers who handle
the craft are now getting into the boat. There are many too

many for the old scow which keeps lurching and pulling off
shore while everyone teeters and straddles. The crowd
pushes toward the shore, expectant, excited.

Said:
   Now they gather at the River.
   The inconsequential, muddy, straight, briney
   Drainage ditch to the Dead Sea.
   Poison. Full of savor.
   Salt's a Christian sign.
   We're preserved in brine!
   One might jump the Jordan
   Even after a spring rain.
   It's uncomfortable
   That the gulch is not more notable,
   At least as wide as the First Heaven!
   The bishop's safely in his boat.
   Now the priests climb in
   Three of them,
   And the Bible and the flowers
   And the staff and vestments.
   There *is* a miracle here.
   The boat's still afloat.
American man:
   Not much to cross over
   Is there?
   It's a bit of a shock,
   That "other shore"
   So near.

American woman:
> Maybe Resurrection
> Is only a newborn turtle
> Digging itself out of the mud.

The boat pushes off to the middle of the river. The priests,
with much tipping, slipping, and changing of places and
Bibles, attend the Bishop:

Bishop:
> THE GREAT BLESSING OF THE WATERS:

The Bishop here dips the Cross into the river three times.
Each time he says:
> Let all adverse powers be crushed beneath the sign of
> the image of the Cross.

First Priest:
> And in that day thou shalt say,
> O Lord, I will praise thee:
> Though thou wast angry with me,
>> Thine anger is turned away, and thou
>> comfortedst me.
> Behold , God is my salvation;
> I will trust, and not be afraid:
> For the Lord Jehovah is my strength and my song
> He also is become my salvation.
> Therefore with joy shall ye draw water
> Out of the wells of salvation.
> And in that day shall ye say,
> Praise the Lord, call upon his name,

Declare his doings among the people,
Make mention that his name is exalted.
Sing unto the Lord; for he hath done excellent things:
This is known in all the earth.
Cry out and shout, thou inhabitant of Zion:
          For great is the Holy One of Israel in the
          midst of thee.

Bishop:
          THE ANNOINTING OF THE WATER:

Third Priest:
          The wilderness and the solitary place shall be glad
                    for them;
          And the desert shall rejoice, and blossom as the rose.
          It shall blossom abundantly, and rejoice
          Even with joy and singing:
          The glory of Lebanon shall be given unto it,
          The excellency of Carmel and Sharon;
          They shall see the glory of the Lord,
          And the excellency of our God.
          Strengthen ye the weak hands,
          And confirm the feeble knees.
          Say to them that are of a fearful heart,Be strong, fear
                    not:
          Behold, your God will come with vengeance,
          Even God with a recompense;
          He will come and save you.
          Then the eyes of the blind shall be opened,
          And the ears of the deaf shall be unstopped.
          Then shall the lame man leap as a hart,

And the tongue of the dumb sing:
For in the wilderness shall waters break out,
And streams in the desert.
And the parched ground shall become a pool,
And the thirsty land springs of water:
In the habitation of dragons, where each lay,
Shall be grass with reeds and rushes.
And a highway shall be there, and a way,
And it shall be called The Way of Holiness;
The unclean shall not pass over it; but it shall be for
        those:
The wayfaring men, though fools, shall not err
        therein.
No lion shall be there,
Nor any ravenous beast shall go up thereon,
It shall not be found there;
But the ransomed of the Lord shall return,
And come to Zion with songs
And everlasting joy upon their heads:
They shall obtain joy and gladness,
And sorrow and sighing shall flee away.

Rifaat:

Beware insomnia
Plead, plead, plead,
Till you drop…
Down, down, down.
Sinless sleep.
Sweet sleep.

American woman:

Wadiah! You've got to stop them.
It's pagan.

Wadiah:
      The cock would crow.
Here a priest empties the jar of oil into a bowl and holds it
for the Bishop. The Bishop dips the flowers into the oil
three times, each time sprinkling the oil on the water as he
sings slowly:
      Alleluia, Alleluia, Alleluia.

Said:

      The dust is quiet and still
      On the hill.

American woman: (her tone has changed to outrage)
      I understand the symbolism
      Alpha and Omega and all that,
      Even immersion
      Of a man in his prime,
      Or a girl
      In a shallow, clean, pool.
      But not in something slippery with salt.
      This! This is a high wire act.
      Daring God. Accusing.
      It's blasphemy!

Wadiah:
      The cock would crow!

Rifaat:

Up to Shiloh with a lamb
Down to Jordan with a lamb.
Down. Down. Down.

Second Priest:
>   Ho, every one that thirsteth, come ye to the waters,
        And he that hath no money;
        Come ye, buy, and eat;
        Yea, come, buy wine and milk
        Without money and without price.
        Wherefore do ye spend money for that which is
                not bread?
        And your labor for that which satisfieth not?
        Hearken diligently unto me, and eat ye that which is
                good,
        And let your soul delight itself in fatness.
        Incline your ear, and come unto me:
        Hear, and your soul shall live;
        And I will make an everlasting covenant with you,
        Even the sure mercies of David.
        Behold, I have given him for a witness to the people,
        A leader and commander to the people.
        Behold, thou shalt call a nation that thou knowest
                not
        And nations that knew not thee shall run unto thee,
        Because of the Lord thy God,
        And for the Holy One of Israel; for he hath glorified
                thee,
        Seek ye the Lord while he may be found,
        Call ye upon him while he is near:
        Let the wicked forsake his way,

And the unrighteous man his thoughts:
And let him return unto the Lord, and he will have
        mercy upon him;
And to our God, for he will abundantly pardon.
For my thoughts are not your thoughts,
Neither are your ways my ways, saith the Lord.
For as the heavens are higher than the earth,
So are my ways higher than your ways,
And my thoughts than your thoughts.
For as the rain cometh down,
And the snow from heaven,
And returneth not thither,
But watereth the earth,
And maketh it bring forth and bud,
That it may give seed to the sower, and bread to the
        eater:
So shall my word be that goeth forth out of my
        mouth:
It shall not return unto me void,
But it shall accomplish that which I please,
And it shall prosper in the thing whereto I sent it.
For ye shall go out with joy,
And be led forth with peace:
The mountains and the hills shall break forth before
        you into singing,
And all the trees of the field shall clap their hands.
Instead of the thorn shall come up the fir tree,
And instead of the brier shall come up the myrtle tree:
And it shall be to the Lord for a name,
For an everlasting sign that shall not be cut off.

The boat then comes in to shore slowly, almost capsizing
once as the priests try to find a place for the Bible and to
make room for the baby. Mona and Ramon walk toward it
with the baby Majed in Ramon's arms.

American man:

        Wadiah! This is a baby.
        Cults, symbols, crosses,
        They're all right if you don't take
        Someone else's chances.
        My God, woman, stop this circus!

Wadiah:

        We came out from Egypt
        From the green womb
        The gold tomb.
        Lot chose Sodom.
        Abram took the high rock.

Said:

        Crucifixion.
        Asphyxiation.

American man:

        You're gambling on God,
        Seven...come Heaven.

Wadiah:

        La. We know his reward!
        We've tilled its sod.

Said:
> Preserve the corpse in the Dead Sea.
> Salt's the Christian savor.

American man:
> You're trying magic!

Wadiah:
> Look at the Promised Land.
> Moses died. It's dear!

American man:
> My God! It *is* dear!

The Bishop climbs out of the boat. Ramon presents the child
to him and gives the priest who has accompanied the Bishop
a white cloth   The crowd is silent.

The Bishop:
> THIS IS THE OIL OF GLADNESS

He touches the child with oil a priest has poured into a bowl:
> on his breast, saying "Unto the healing of body and
> soul.
> On both ears, saying "Unto the hearing of faith"
> On both hands, saying "Thy hands have made and
> fashioned me
> On both feet, saying "That he may walk in the way
> of Thy commandments, O Lord."

The Bishop gives the child back to Ramon. Then, with
much tipping, the Bishop and the priest climb back into the
boat. Again everyone is in the boat with Bibles, Cross,
soldiers,and flowers . Ramon gives the child, once more,
to the Bishop. The soldiers push the boat off shore
 a short distance The parents kneel to wait.

Rifaat:

      Salt's the savor of blood.

Wadiah:

      It's warm here.

The American woman leaves Wadiah, goes to her husband
who has moved away.

American woman:

      They're so literal…
      He who saveth his life…
      So they brandish a knife.
      Present your living bodies!
      They don't use reason
      In life, or love, or death.

Rifaat:

      When the time was come
      He steadfastly set his face…

(When the boat has steadied and come to a standstill,with the
help of a priest, the bishop grasps the baby by the wrists,…
Then he holds the baby out by the wrists over the water and
submerges him three times, saying:

The child of God is baptized
In the name of the Father (first dip)
And of the Son (second dip)
And of the Holy Ghost (third dip)
(while women in the crowd ululate, Mona makes a
movement and chokes)
Music off stage: "Listen to the lambs… All are crying"

Each time he is submerged,the child pulls his knees up under
his chin, gasping, but not crying. As the baby comes up for
the third time, Mona and Ramon smile. Then they cup their
hands, scooping the river into them, and drink the muddy
water.

As they rise the whole crowd pushes to the river's edge for
its share of the holy water. They use their hands for cups,
or tin cups, or empty gazooze bottles, and pass it around like
a chalice of wine.

Said:

Drink ye all of it. (with deep revulsion)
Humanity's hung up,
Drunk,
In a river of blood.
Ugh.

The women continue to ululate and the priests and people
finally join in a chant of praise which swells as the boat
rocks.

The Bishop wraps the baby in the white wrapping Mona has
given him.

Bishop:
> The child of God is clothed with a garment of
> Righteousness, with a robe of Light.

The soldiers begin to row the boat toward shore.

Said:
> Having received the vinegar...

Rifaat:
> God waded into Jordan
> And we lost him.

(silence now hangs over the holy moment)

Said:
> Up on a cross.
> Even Jesus
> Didn't come here
> Until he was a man.

American woman:
> Look at them.
> That woman
> Let her little son
> Share his cup with the blind man.
> He has trachoma.

American man:
        Are they ignorant,
        Or desperate?

American woman:
        This whole country
        Makes me uneasy.
        I can't help realizing
        Every time we wind down
        From Jerusalem,
        How that certain man
        Could have been a snare
        To catch some simpleton
        Do-gooder
        Unaware.

American man:
        If this went on at the Mississippi
        It …

Rifaat:
        Push to the river.
        The baby pulls them down.

American woman:
        It's all so ignominious.
        Even the Way of the Cross:
        Golgotha!
        Doesn't take five minutes
        To walk

The whole distance.
I'm faint from homesickness,
For the Arthurian legend,
For a horse and a cause,
Some gallantry,
And a coat of mail.

Said:

Watch the Americans.
Reason is green wood.
It won't ignite.
Their spark has gone out.
Wadiah should have known.
Usually she knows
What to keep to herself
Or among her own.

American man:

The dogs barking
Will tear us raw
Before we get home.

Rifaat:

Having received the vinegar,
He gave up the Ghost.

Said:

The River
Is only a spring-swollen creek
But the stick
Standing knee deep

In the stinking water
Is green all summer.

The boat touches shore.

The Bishop gives the baby to Ramon. Then one soldier
helps the Bishop, then the priest to step out of the boat. As
the last priest steps ashore, the soldier loses his balance and
leaps feet first into the waist deep water. The boat lurches,
but the soldier is helped by the other, and they together
steady the scow at shore.

The Bishop:
On shore, the Bishop again takes Majed from Ramon.
Drawing from his cassock, where it has been safe-guarded
close to his heart, the Bishop brings forth a small alabaster
or silver vial which contains the most precious oil, oil sent
directly through the Patriarch to the Bishop. With this oil he
once more annoints the child. This time, he makes the Sign
of the Cross with each drop of oil he pours on the child's
body.

Bishop:
        (Anointing Majed's brow)
        "The seal of the gift of the Holy Spirit",

Wadiah: standing beside Mona, her black eyes, her
furrowed brows attending the Bishop eagle -sharp
        SEAL.

Bishop:

(Anointing Majed's eyes)
"The seal of the gift of the Holy Spirit",

Wadiah:
SEAL.

Bishop:
(Anointing Majed's nostrils)
"The seal of the gift of the Holy Spirit",

Wadiah:
SEAL.

Bishop:
(Anointing Majed's lips)
"The seal of the gift of the Holy Spirit",

Wadiah:
SEAL.

Bishop:
(Anointing both ears)
"The seal of the gift of the Holy Spirit",

Wadiah:
SEAL.

Bishop:
(Anointing Majed's breast)
"The seal of the gift of the Holy Spirit",

Wadiah:
>SEAL.

Bishop:
>(Anointing both hands)
>"The seal of the gift of the Holy Spirit",

Wadiah:
>SEAL.

Bishop:
>(Anointing both feet.)
>"The seal of the gift of the Holy Spirit".

Wadiah:
>SEAL.

Next, the Bishop takes a sponge from the first priest who has dipped it into the river and tenderly washes the child's whole head and body. Then, he performs the final act of the Baptism:

The Bishop:
>THE TONSURE,
>THE CHILD OF GOD'S FIRST SACRIFICE:

The Bishop, receiving scissors from the second priest, cuts the childs's hair.

Second Priest:

> What shall we say then? Shall we continue in sin,
> that grace may abound? God forbid. How shall we,
> that are dead to sin, live any longer therein? Know
> ye not that so many of us as were baptized into Jesus
> Christ were baptized into his death? Therefore we are
> buried with him by baptism into death: that like as
> Christ was raised up from the dead,by the glory of
> the Father, even so we also should walk in newness
> of life. For if we have been planted together in the
> likeness of his death, we shall be also in the likeness
> of his resurrection.

Third Priest:

> Go ye therefore, and teach all nations, baptizing them
> in the name of the Father, and of the Son, and of the
> Holy Ghost: Teaching them to observe all things
> whatsoever I have commanded you: and lo, I am
> with you alway, even unto the end of the world.

> At last, the Bishop places Majed into Mona's waiting
> arms. Smiling and full of joy, she and Ramon
> meander off together bowed over their bundle,
> comforting and cuddling him, to the sunny field
> down right of stage where they sit on a rock, dry
> Majed, and dress him, wrapping him now in the
> American woman's blanket. They play with him as
> though he is very special, a blessed child.

Ramon: (pointing up toward the rear right balcony)
> See the Jerusalem tower.

It's not so far.
If we have hope,
We have cheer.

The bishop and priests walk back up the aisle they came
down. The crowd breaks up quickly and goes off stage.
Everyone is casual. The Americans move a bit left of center
and spread a picnic on the river bank. Wadiah is left alone.
She looks drained now, of spirit, and tired.

Wadiah: (clicks her tongue and tosses her head in a quick
negating motion)
   La'!
   No dove.
(She turns and moves slowly down the steps, crosses over
to the left and up another stair to the stage where her ironing
board stands ready. She rights the shirt on the board and
begins to fuss with the iron.)

Said:
   Cain's offering.
   It only smoldered.

Rifaat:
   Up to Shiloh with a lamb
   Down to Jordan with a lamb.

American man:
   My God!
   Piety spreads like a flame on gasoline.
   Like Hell fire.

American woman.

>Did you watch Wadiah?
>She flung her head higher
>And didn't wince or shed a tear.
>Just stood
>Impaled on her faith..

American man:

>God! Love's dear here.
>It *was* only a lamb,
>Just a smudge of wool in fire.

>Now it's Mona's baby…or ours. That living
>sacrifice!

Rifaat:

>Seaweed knots thick and tight
>In the lap of God.
>Love is greedy.
>Tangles the baby
>Pulls it down, down.

Said:

>Oh you were the hero!
>You wouldn't get tangled.
>You'd go to school
>You'd chance your life to learn.
>Then you'd come back,
>Make *our* desert bloom.
>My God I'm sick of that phrase.

Feed the hungry,
Free the wise, and bring the wealthy low.
The hero's hung on a thorn.

Rifaat:

You're Caught.
Bound for good.
Jesus I love this niche.
You, there,
Cringe in your Father's lap.
Still, or he'll dump you out.

Said:

From Abram's high rock
All washes down, turns to salt.
On Judah's height,
Cautiousness is wisdom.

Rifaat:

Risk is freedom.

Said:

Freedom's not for man.

Rifaat:

Leap, leap out of your Father's lap.

Said:

He's dumped me out.

Rifaat:

Lie flat on the mud floor,

Feel its cool on your belly.

Said:

Catch a cold and die.

Rifaat:

Lie with a woman.

Said:

Love's a muddy river, man,
With no dowry.

Rifaat:

Go ahead. Drown.
Drown in the sum sound
Round Omega.
I have a sociology class now.
   The Scapegoat,
   Rifa'at

Said:

You can't sign off with that!
What's this about Scapegoat?
Wadiah didn't send you off for Isaac.
She meant to save *you*.
Remember how she went to Chile
After her big argument with Omar?
She came back, though.
She knows who she is.
I've decided this is the way.
I'm in it for life,
Bound for good, I'll stay
Here. I might catch Wadiah's courage.

165

Leaving my pile of rocks,
I'm entering Bir Zeit in August.

The university's always a target, though,
Like a water source. But, yes, I'll drown.

Wadiah irons furiously. Moody.

Maid: (comes to Wadiah with the American baby.)
      When will Mr. and Mrs. Rich be back?

Wadiah: (stoic)
      They stayed for a picnic.

Maid:

      Robert's cried all morning.
      Could you take him while I do their rooms?

Wadiah: (going right on ironing, not looking up)
      They might not want me to.

Maid:

      Was it nice today?

Wadiah:

      La' (with the upward, negative toss of her head)

Maid:

      Did Majed cry?
      (bemused, with the American baby in her arms)
      They always do,

And pull their little legs up,
As if they try to be unborn.
Can't though,
Once you've started out.
Wadiah:
I don't deserve a dove.
I want too much.   Ramon,
Maybe he should run away, like Rifaat.

Maid:
Come, Wadiah, take him.
He'll stop whimpering.
You're his love.
Please, Wadiah, do.
Wadiah:
La'! I'd duck him in the river.

But she puts the iron down and, taking the baby, she sits in
a straight chair to cuddle him. The baby, enveloped in her
arms and bosom, nestles comfortable. The maid goes out.
Wadiah begins to sing "Alleluia" like a lullaby. In spite of
herself, she grows cheerful as she holds the baby.

American woman (still at the picnic)
Promised Land!
It's not much of a bargain
For all that wandering.
It's not even natural.
Look, here's a gazooze bottle,
There's a banana skin,
It's like July 5th at Manasquan.

American man:
> This morning was unnerving.
> I'm sick of it.
> What if we stop and pick up a reservation
> Tonight,… get on back
> To Philadelphia.

American woman:
> And shut out all this religiosity
> And superstition,… the blind beggars,
> And every scarfed head.
> There's no real hope of seeing Rifaat.

Said: (Turning to the Americans)
> All Strangers.
> Expecting milk and honey,
> Expecting giant cedars,
> A clear blue river and welling springs…
> What *they* think they're promised.
> The Chosen's blood
> Salts our sea.
> It poisons us.

American woman:
> I'm sure he prefers
> That we give Wadiah a gift.
> He must worry about her.
> This senseless ritual!
> That frightening ululation.
> I can't get it out of my ears.

She begins to gather up the picnic things.

American man:
        No rules.
        No limits.
        No wonder they can't run governments.
        They all speak in hyperbole.

Said
        On Mars Hill…

Wadiah: (To the baby who is whimpering again)
        You will go too.
        I'll be alone,
        Shut outside a wall,
        A soldier with a gun stands
        At the post office door.
        Next year, Mrs. Greene brings her children.
        Then I'll cry when they're gone.
        Cuddle down, cuddle down.
        Sleep… sleep.

She begins to walk the baby, happy again, singing.

Said:
        Passover.The angel
        Hasn't seen the blood
        On our lintels.
        Drowned.
        The sea rolled in. On us.

American woman (coming downstage to the steps)
        I get a headache every time
        We come near this sea.
        It's the depressing humidity,
        It's so muggy.

Said:
        Love's muggy.

American man:
        Did you know that only algae,
         And little of that,
        Can live in the Dead Sea?

The Americans go on out the aisle.

Mona: (Holding Majed close)
        I didn't know why.
        I thought, before, it was for resurrection.
        Now I see it is to drown,
        To drown in love…
        The gift of the Magi.
        The gift of Christ.
Ramon:
        Love makes no promises:
        No dove,
        No land.
        We'd better start up.
        Those Jerusalem towers

Seem nearer than they are.
I'm getting hungry
And (he touches Majed, smiling) so is he.

Ramon and Mona start up the aisle. Ramon carries Majed

Said (climbing down from his ladder)
        Sacer ficare. God's miracle.
        On the High Place
        In Omega's sum sound,
        The stone altar pinwheels,
        Spins the cross-spokes of its grill,
        Scapegoats, lambs and doves sizzle.

        Strange. They spatter hope onto the low places.
        Its smoke wafts sweet incense.

        Drown. Go down in the ululation
        Circling from where you're dunked in.
        Gasp. Grasp the water and pull it down.
        Let it, and the Jordan will raise you up.

        I'll take the wadi* footpath home.
        Wish you were here to walk with me.
        Do come home. Soon.
                        With Love,
                        Said

Wadi: A very deep glen; Said's leads from Jericho and the
Jordan River up to Jerusalem. It will be a dark valley by the
time he reaches the Holy City.

PRESENTING A LIVING SACRIFICE
A HANDSHAKE, PEACE

Their bread gone, their water gone,
Ishmaels grope through this gorge,
Their scripture measure (no less- no more)
Shadowing the way, darkening
Crevices where scorpions lie, sharpening
Any stone jut.

Straining, their ears turn, hurting, toward
Their hope for the Shepherd's fluting call,
Smarting, their eyes search for the well,
For the green pastures, for the plenty,
The staff, even His rod would be a mercy,
For the table prepared
In the house of the Lord.

Not bargaining, disdaining usury,
They share the last of their lentils
With beggars who touch their hearts' tendrils.
Like foxfire they glow steadily, undimmed,
Like fire-flies, they star
The dark of the mind. On an enemy's head,
They flame Pentecosts.
We dream we smell the incense, faintly.
We wait.

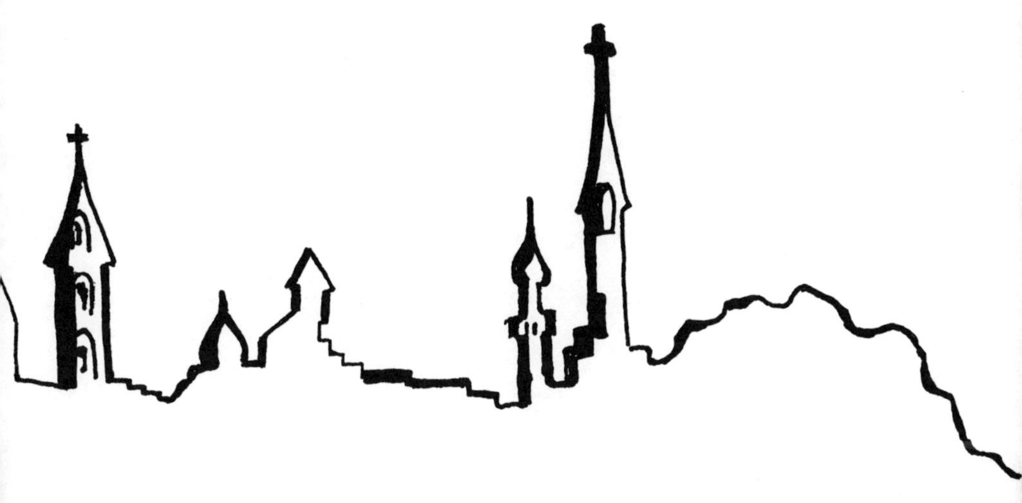

God is our Lord and your Lord.
We have our deeds, and you have your deeds;
There is no argument between us and you;
God shall bring us together, and unto Him is
the homecoming.

        Qur'an XLII